The Graduate Institute for World Affairs/   Number 4

France and the European Community

A Publication of the Mershon Center for Education in National Security

France and the European Community

Edited by Sydney Nettleton Fisher

Ohio State University Press

The Graduate Institute for World Affairs

1/ THE MILITARY IN THE MIDDLE EAST
Problems in Society and Government
Edited by Sydney Nettleton Fisher

2/ SYRIAN POLITICS AND THE MILITARY
1945–1958
By Gordon H. Torrey

3/ EXPLOSIVE FORCES IN LATIN AMERICA
Edited by John J. TePaske and Sydney Nettleton Fisher

Preface

THE PAPERS contained in this volume were presented at the third annual three-day conference of the Graduate Institute for World Affairs of the Ohio State University, October 24-26, 1963. The announced general theme was "France and the European Community." There were four formal sessions, each with two papers, and invited discussion leaders initiated the open and public comment on, and consideration of, the points of view advanced by the authors. As can be imagined, the papers aroused controversy and elicited forceful arguments in defense of particular topics and theses. The several authors have benefited from these exchanges and have been able to incorporate some of the ideas growing out of the discussions in their papers when preparing them for publication.

Because of varying schedules, other commitments, and transportation problems, the papers were not delivered in the same order in which they are arranged in this volume. At the opening session, chaired by Professor Edgar S. Furniss, Jr., Director of the Social Science Program of the Mershon Center for Education in National Security of the Ohio State University, Professors Pounds and Knorr read their papers, and discussions were led by Mr. Robert C. Doty, of the *New York Times,* and Colonel DeWitt C. Armstrong III, of the Policy Planning Council of the Department of State.

The second session was opened by Ambassador Winthrop G. Brown, Deputy Commandant for Foreign Affairs of the National

War College, who introduced Dr. Minneman and Dr. Diebold. Comments on their papers were made by Professor Elmer W. Learn, of the Department of Agricultural Economics at the University of Minnesota, and Professor Herbert S. Parnes, of the Department of Economics at the Ohio State University.

At the third session, which was led by Dean Lester G. Crocker of the Graduate School of Western Reserve University, Professors Demorest and Schmitt presented their papers. The discussion leaders at this session were Professor Georges N. Joyaux, of the Department of Modern Languages at Michigan State University, and Professor Edward W. Fox, of the Department of History at Cornell University.

The final session was chaired by Professor S. William Halperin, of the Department of History at the University of Chicago and the editor of the *Journal of Modern History*. Professors Fulda and Brzezinski delivered their papers at this session, and the discussions were opened by Professor Peter Hay, of the College of Law at the University of Illinois, and Professor Robert F. Byrnes, of the Department of History and the Russian Institute at Indiana University.

Following the conference, the eight authors revised and expanded their papers to include important details and material that the shortage of time had forced them to exclude from the oral versions. Editing of the essays has been kept to a minimum since the authors themselves spontaneously eliminated digressions—perhaps because of the distinguished character of the audience.

The authors wish to indicate here their indebtedness to the chairmen of the sessions, the leaders of the discussions, and many others in attendance at the conference for their valuable and pertinent public and private comments. All of the contributors to this volume seem in agreement that many of the most valuable ideas generated by the conference evolved during the more intimate conversations and exchanges among participants that took place during the three days of the conference.

SYDNEY NETTLETON FISHER

Contents

Tables

Abbreviations Used in the Text and Notes

BeNeLux ...... Belgium-Netherlands-Luxembourg
Customs Union
CAP .... Common Agricultural Policy
CEMA .... Council for Economic Mutual Assistance
CPSU .... Communist Party of the Soviet Union
EAEC (Euratom) European Atomic Energy Community
ECE .... Economic Commission for Europe
ECSC .... European Coal and Steel Community
EDC .... European Defense Community
EEC .... European Economic Community
EFTA .... European Free Trade Association
ENI .... Ente Nazionale Idrocarburi
GATT .... General Agreement on Tariffs and Trade
GDR .... German Democratic Republic
GNP .... Gross national product
MLF .... (European) Multilateral Nuclear Force
MRP .... Mouvement Republicain Populaire
NATO .... North Atlantic Treaty Organization
OEEC .... Organization of European Economic
Co-operation
SAC .... Strategic Air Command
UDSR .... Union Democratique et Sociale de la Resistance
UNR .... Union pour la Nouvelle République

France and the European Community

French Culture and the European Community: The Complexity of Survival   JEAN-JACQUES DEMOREST

IN THE LIGHT of the so-called European crisis—a crisis aggravated in America by a combination of legitimate impatience and of transparent calculation—there is perhaps a virtue in presenting a moral portrait of France, a hasty survey of the mental and cultural temper of the nation today. The following appraisal, expressed in terms not only alien but unpalatable to well-bred political scientists, unavoidably poses more problems than it solves. In keeping with the topic, thorny France and its inflexible prophet, it is appropriate to take the liberty of adopting an unbending tone, for in the domain of ideas and literature the most valid approach is one based on sympathy, on a certain degree of emotive identification with the subject at hand.

Before the late war a few little points of discord separated France and Germany. In the ensuing polemics, the French made a capital discovery: they conceded that the Germans, poor obfuscated Knights of the Forget-me-not, might have had at one time—say, up to the death of Nietzsche, or up to 1914—a *Kultur*, but the French, oh wonder!, had something infinitely superior: a civilization, *la civilisation française*. Now the distinction between the two is not entirely one of acrobatic sophistry; it is real. But given the impossibility of translating into English all the shadings implied by the notion of *civilisation*, it is better to become reconciled to the term *culture*, while informing it with the values inherent in *civilisation*.

In any case, *culture* fits one immediate aspect of the complexities to be broached implying as it does four prerequisites: seed, earth, roots, and care. Seed, in other words, the existence of a fruit-bearing past. Earth, the existence of a concrete, localized humus not afforded by the glass and steel hothouse of the United Nations. Roots, the existence of a life-giving rooting in the peculiar reality of a nation's being, not in the rarified atmosphere of sublime international abstractions. Care, the patience of time and love, not the fumbling fever of hurried alliances.

Now then, looking at the title chosen for this essay, a humanist might well scoff at the apparent contradiction. An economic community and culture, really! Urbane brigandage and philosophy! Chickens and Baudelaire! Come, my good man, what have they in common? A great deal. The French and every other nation have sought in technical advances a partial paliative to Paul Valéry's anguished warning of the 1930's: "Les civilisations sont mortelles." The last thirty years have taught all peoples that the perennial quality of national art forms and idioms is not assured. Cultures are fragile, constantly menaced from within and from without. Nations pathetically survive the slow agony of their cultures.

One may go a bit further and ask whether a nation can remain intellectually dynamic and spiritually creative without possessing power. Does one know of any such example in history? Do not the periods when France, linguistically and culturally, led the civilized world coincide exactly with those of her technical mastery? Is, then, the price of a flourishing culture too great when it must be paid by a high degree of technical prowess and of political independence? De Gaulle insists that the price is not too great, and France concurs. But does not the world, and specifically the United States, find the price exorbitant, rife with danger? That is quite another question.

When did France lose that technical mastery which she so cruelly missed in 1940? When did she first neglect to launch wholeheartedly into industrialization? Who was responsible? Arnold Toynbee blames Napoleon and *la gloire*. But Mr. Toynbee is somewhat of an Englishman, and his nation was quite maligned

4

when it was erroneously caricatured by John Bull's belly. In reality, the English—bless them all—would best be represented by an elephant; not so much because they are a wise, primeval, slow-moving giant—which they are—but because they never forget. Bonaparte, alias "Boney," is still stuck in their throats—certainly in Mr. Toynbee's, whose profession is precisely not to forget. It seems improper, however, to ascribe to Napoleon, who often enough was faithful to the Revolution, what was originally the French Revolution's responsibility. The day it guillotined Lavoisier, it formalized, and rather dramatically, its already obvious reliance on ideology rather than applied science to liberate the world from tyranny and famine.

This moot point of history is only incidental to the subject at hand. It remains that today as ever—such are the advantages of a long tradition—the French are convinced that in their culture, or rather in its promises for the future, they possess something valuable which the world, and surely Europe, cannot do without. Hence they are pained to learn that the American part of the world, for one, would be delighted to spare them the trouble of acquiring the instruments of absolute power. For barring total multilateral disarmament, a society to stay creative must be in complete possession of its destiny; hence in possession of its own weapons of death. And *ipso facto* a creative society radiates in every direction, obedient to every challenge of the mind, to every wind of human enterprise. It does not specialize in cubism, stuffed truffles, and the cancan. It is perhaps a sorry commentary that the sword is the axis of the world and that power is a tangible that one does not share; but it has always been so. Culture, political independence, military power, and technical inventiveness are closely related factors. The last three are not automatic assurances of culture, but culture cannot survive without them.

Culture as reflected in modern France is not a commodity of pleasure; it is a creative risk. Many, however, tend to confuse it with pleasure: sitting spellbound in a concert hall; tasting an exquisite sauce; laughing in a theater. Culture is more than its consumption. In a way it is dissatisfaction with what has preceded:

resistance and refusal. It is a people's tense awareness of self, of destiny, and the past. An essentially creative consciousness, it takes the shape of a constantly new dialogue between the dead and the living, thinking on the future. This dialogue is to be heard, sung or whispered, by man and nature, in every city, field, and forest. Just as in the religious quest any pause, any relaxation of the intensity is a regression, a fall. This is the price of culture. It allows neither bargaining nor indulgent wavering. Again one may ask: Is it too high? Through its intransigeant president France says it is not.

De Gaulle and France, France and De Gaulle, it is an old love affair, though a reverent one. De Gaulle is even wont to speak of "Notre Dame la France." Yet what is there in common between sunny, graceful France and its dour devotee? More than meets the eye. For De Gaulle was born in Lille, in the vast sad plain of Flanders hard by the Belgian border; and the character of France is not in uniform civility, but in balanced diversity. The ceaseless dialogue mentioned above is not only literary (Montaigne and Pascal, Pascal and Voltaire, Voltaire and Rousseau . . .), it is also social, and De Gaulle allies in his temperament, in his blood, the warring strains of France: the realistic tenacity of the bourgeois on his mother's side and the haughty idealism of the aristocrat on his father's side; catholicism and socialism; faith and liberalism; classicism and romanticism; tradition and revolution. Perhaps in him, and in France, these dialectic forces are slowly being resolved. Perhaps he will succeed where Napoleon failed: in marrying tradition and revolution—this not simply by dint of genius, but because of the weight of time, the inevitable play of circumstances, and the wearing-down of tired frictions. From that point of view one cannot stress too strongly the significance of the presence in De Gaulle's cabinet of that nostalgic bard of Death, Eros, and Revolution, the novelist André Malraux. The fervent commitment implied by Malraux's active participation in the cabinet underscores the pre-eminent role that culture plays in De Gaulle's outlook; otherwise, Malraux would have returned long since to his anguished contemplation of man as he reads him in the smiling angel of the Rheims cathedral or in the dark blood of Goya's brush.

In any event the image of France that most have nurtured as a whimsical, comely maiden, skipping once to the left, once to the right, as she progresses in time, may be slightly distorted if, as Charles Péguy asserted, a revolution is the movement of a less perfect tradition toward a more perfect one.

At this point one is quite warranted in questioning the sanity of the present argument. What is the theme being discussed: De Gaulle, the future of Gaullist dreams, or French culture? The radical distinction or the positive equation of these two elements is the basic problem. Just as in the political realm the essential question to be faced is whether or not De Gaulle is France.

Does Gaullist policy reflect a lasting attitude of French culture? It does. Or at least, it reflects *one* of the lasting French attitudes. After all, a living, expanding culture is multiform. Based on a sustained opposition of contradictory positions, its validity can be measured in part by the capacity to provoke and maintain inner clashes. Uniformity, on the other hand, indicates attrition. The present "isolation" of France is somewhat tactical; it is not the expression of a culture that has severed with the world so much as one in the process of sizing itself up, tightening its muscles before a new challenge. What one observes today in France is a phase of the total picture. Nevertheless, this phase belongs to a permanent pattern. Embodied in De Gaulle and endowed with political articulation, it should be treated simultaneously as only one of the constants of French culture and yet as the dominant one at the present. Hence one is justified in analyzing De Gaulle's objectives as those of French culture. It is not necessarily a binding choice or a personal commitment, so much as a well-grounded option, a realistic perspective. The plain fact is that in its active majority the French nation has espoused a rather determined Gaullist outlook.

Moreover, the equation between a man and a national heritage, this mystical correspondence and identification, so alien in many respects to the Anglo-Saxon temper (though there is close by the example of Winston Churchill who was England's soul and history more perfectly than the aggregate of his contemporaries, just as Lincoln was in his time), this communion between a personality and a culture is not only compatible with the French spirit, but is one of its marks, one of its profoundly human attractions. Little matters what its historical origins may be, whether or not one elects to trace it to a certain nostalgia for the monarchial past perceptible even in the working classes. It is one of those perennial traits, now dominant, with which the world must reckon. It bears a name: "la Mystique." Born as a political concept in the late nineteenth century, it can be more readily associated with the Catholic left than with the right. It is illusive and inherently dangerous; but after all, everything deeply human is a passionate gamble, a deliberate peril.

This belief, this desire for a mystique, is in itself but one aspect of the irrational side of the French cultural dialogue. The other side, perhaps more monolithic, is logic; for the French people have a mania or a genius, as one would have it, for lucidity and reason. The two confronted in sustained combat create that balanced diversity already mentioned. Here again in De Gaulle, who is clearly imbued with the spirit of French classicism yet who is romantic in imagination and ideals, the two elements are tautly entwined.

Fine, agreed; but as one hears from all sectors, Why has France abdicated her rebellious spirit to this man? Why indeed, if not that after three generations of parliamentary clowning and of paper figureheads, the French yearn for a political and cultural reality. They are tired of anonymity. They want to hear a real voice, a recognizable one, even if it does break on those infernal high notes of the "Marseillaise." As for France's abdicating her rebellious spirit, Washington and London are aware that such is not the case.

De Gaulle and his France did not pop up *ex nihilo*. Where specifically, to what intellectual and spiritual movement, can the present Gaullist attitudes be linked? Mainly to that group of inspired and dedicated poets, novelists, and polemists who are responsible for the renewal and broadening of the religious experience in France. They have sometimes been defined by the famous cry of one of them who was asked by an exasperated critic exactly what sort of a man he might be. To which he answered vociferously: "Un pèlerin de l'absolu"—"a pilgrim of the absolute." This inflexible definition suits De Gaulle's France. Léon Bloy, Charles Péguy, Georges Bernanos, and Paul Claudel were such pilgrims. Today, André Malraux could be loosely tied to them, as could the Catholic novelist François Mauriac. De Gaulle's France probably owes most to Charles Péguy. The very image of uncompromising civic integrity and of poetic charity, Péguy fell during the battle of the Marne in 1914, forever embraced by the "terre charnelle" for which he sang and prayed. More intimately yet, De Gaulle befriended the prophetic Bernanos for a while before his death in 1948, as he does today Malraux and Mauriac.[1]

The greatness of poetry, a greatness largely unheeded by scientists, historians, or statesmen, is that everything it imagines has happened or will happen. Its visions precede the discoveries of science, while its ideals orient and mold the course of politics. De Gaulle likes to put it this way: "Tout se tient." As far as human intelligence comprehends, the universe is held together by endless analogy. In its hidden rhythm, an eternal rhythm which the poet briefly seizes then loses, a smile rhymes with a man to be, with a lost planet, with an obsolete law, with a future war. And so it was that forty-four years after Péguy's death, the nation wended its way along the path of the pilgrims of the absolute, stumbling as a nation would, cursing, swearing, yet marching just the same. This does not mean that De Gaulle is necessarily the man the prophets called for, the predestined soldier-poet-saint-sinner that they wanted; but he is, for better or for worse, the man who, consciously or unconsciously, answered their call.

What characterized these four absolutists? They were the prey of the same anguish, burned by the same thirst. Men for whom the Word was Action, men who hardly asked any other questions than those which concerned and challenged the total being. Dreamers committed to the here and now, visionaries hungry for concrete reality, their lucidity was as penetraating as their imagination was vast.

What was their message? First, that there is an absolute, an ultimate reality that is both here and elsewhere, man's reality, so compelling its light blinds; yet the trajectory of intelligence must always aim at the essential, at an elementary grasping of conscious-ness as individuals or as a people. (This De Gaulle does. He completely ignores the unessential. Matters which bedevil other statesmen he simply brushes off as trivial.) Second, this same blinding light converts reality into truth, which is ambiguity. This ambiguity must be admitted and espoused, this interpenetration of flesh and spirit, of clarity and mystery, which children know so well and which Péguy called Entirety. To deny one of the terms of such an inherent ambiguity is to reduce existence, to become a lie. (De Gaulle nurtures ambiguity in state affairs just as he recommends a constant readiness for maneuverability in military affairs. Mobility for him is of the essence; hence he shuns alliances and rigid systems which might reduce the nation's physical and spiritual ability to move.) Third, this basic ambiguity corresponds with an infinity which is here. Therefore, as seen above, all knowl-edge stems from universal analogy: *tout se tient,* any commitment—and man must commit himself—is *de facto* a spiritual commitment. Salvation is collective rather than personal. A statesman does not only play his soul but that of his people as well. Yet play he must, for man is not expected to shelter himself but constantly to create—in other words, to risk himself. The adventure is infinity, the stakes greater than mere physical survival. Lastly, the world is one of adorable complexity. Man is not delegated to simplify it, but to enrich it, to complicate it.

Is this a compendium of what France and her elite believe and practice today? Of course not, though the last point, that of a complexity to be guarded and fostered, is fundamental to all phases of French culture. Moreover, two parts of this poetic credo, namely, the notions of ambiguity and commitment, would satisfy most existentialists on the non-spiritual, ethical plane. However, if the absolutists represent the generation of the 1920's now "come to power," Camus and Sartre represents the generation of the 40's yet to find a voice in government, and those who might be called the experimentalists represent today's generation of the 60's. Such a time gap between the elaboration of an ethical stance and its realization in the political conduct of a nation is not peculiar to France: it simply is more striking in a people whose intellectual adventures are directly instrumental in determining national policy. Here, again, the analyst is confronted with the energy of literature, with the priority in time of the poetic experience over the political. And lest one judge that the influence of literature is exaggerated and that of science neglected, it should be emphasized that literature does enjoy even in the eyes of scientists a pre-eminent position in France. Her distinguished scientists usually have been either great writers (Descartes, Pascal) or at least men who sought and succeeded in being consummately articulate (Claude Bernard, Henri Poincaré, Teilhard de Chardin). France has always expected of the scientist that he address himself to the layman and that he do so in a clear, imaginative tongue.

As for the young experimentalists' debt to the pilgrims of the absolute, they are only concerned with the notion of ambiguity, but a-religious and desacralized. They illustrate curiously, and at times in a fascinating manner, the technical impetus of contemporary France. Characteristically, even this domain of the nation's activity is reflected in the culture—a culture which in this case is nearly an anti-culture since the experimentalists seek to rid objects of man, to combat the anthropocentric, to objectify emotions and ideas to the point of rendering them as inanimate exchangeable parts. This is true of the technicians of the new novel (Robbe-Grillet, Butor, Nathalie Sarraute) and the technicians of the absurd in the theater (Ionesco, Adamov, and to a lesser degree Beckett and Genet). Considering their obsession with artistic techniques, most of these experimentalists, however, are not likely to be heeded in public affairs, since their opinions are voiced too seldom to have a bearing on the political problems at hand.

Thus if something could be termed the general state of French culture, it would include the basic elements of the credo just discussed; particularly, risk and commitment, ambiguity and its correlative, a rich, complex world. This implies not static policy but new ventures. As a counterforce to these basically romantic traits, there stands the perennial French sense of proportion. Simultaneous with the inclination to view the gigantic as a morbid, pathological phenomenon, whether it be in a mammoth nation or in a mammoth alliance, there is a positive attraction among many Frenchmen for the Third Force as something aesthetically pleasing, logical, and politically viable. Hand in hand with this sense of proportion, or rather this tendency toward a dialectical geometry of ideas, goes an earthiness which still marks France as the China of the West. In this realm the original meaning of culture takes root. The Frenchman's innate sense of the dignity and reality of human rooting leads him to hate abstraction as a modern form of tyranny—a tyranny which reduces the genius of a people into complexes, replacing the concrete experience and personality of a nation, of a *patrie*, with an esoteric, supranational ideology which in turn is but ignorance and sloth in disguise. Needless to say, the United Nations and its acolytes are the favorite targets for such a scorn. This xenophobic abhorrence for simplification is the instinctive response of a highly developed culture which fears for its very existence and shudders at the idea of a world ruled by Freudian psychosociologists (in no other country, unless it be Italy, has Freud been so ignored or lampooned), by Asian McGuffeys, and other grimacing species of UNESCO mass-media fauna.

This arrogant but still very healthy disdain conceals an anxiety. France cannot help tracing the oversimplified vision of world organization back to America, and specifically, to its professional educationalists. Not only is it alien to the temperament of France, but it strains her relations with America. What the French first interpreted as the good-humored gaucherie of a young nation, they have now been led to consider a cunning and perverse form of willful naïveté. Consequently, many Frenchmen are delighted to hear De Gaulle say *Non* or to hear him refer to the United Nations Organization as *le machin*, the thingamajig.

Such are, curtly summarized and malignantly oriented, the banal but active patterns of French culture at work in the nation. Perhaps the description of those patterns as responding to a balanced diversity should be construed as sometimes balanced, always diverse and divergent.

Now to the crux of the matter. Are these patterns, these obsessions and faiths, representative of Europe as well? Is French culture representative of European culture? The answer must be qualified by a temporal factor. During the last thirty years French culture has been, if not wholly European, at least the only moving culture in Europe. Today, at long last, with the reawakening of Italy's artistic vocation and Germany's slow recovery of her cultural personality, things are beginning to change. For the sake of clarity one must dismiss the BeNeLux countries whose size and ambitions perforce limit their role, though they at least succeeded in preserving their soul during the war. But what of Germany and Italy? They lost their culture in the mid-thirties when they reneged their real past and their heritage to impose a false history based on exclusion, pompous fantasy, and hate. The Nazis destroyed the proprietary quality of a slowly emerging German conscience— probably the greatest sin visited on the German people by Hitler. Mussolini did the same with less efficacy. The day that Hitler marched into Salzburg, the child Mozart died. So did German culture, and Europe fell into the throes of agony. Just as Germany, France, and Europe were mysteriously resurrected that summer day in 1944 when De Gaulle, superbly unmindful of the shots still being fired at the nave, walked into the golden *Te Deum* that filled the cathedral of Notre Dame.

European civilization is a delicate being endowed with a sensitive memory and a magnificently uncompromising sense of honor, befitting one knighted in the Middle Ages. It will break at the slightest offense committed against itself. That is why nothing is more pathetic, yet more urgent, than Germany's efforts today to find her soul, as she struggles to reach the mystic clearing beyond the ominous forest of blast furnaces and refineries.

13

In the meantime De Gaulle has taken an equivocal stand: to safeguard Europe by promoting France and to assume that he speaks for the Europe of tomorrow. He is confident that if the Germans and the Italians are more open than the French to the partial loss of identity seemingly implied by the American conception of the Atlantic Alliance, it is precisely because they broke with their cultural roots in the evil years of Hitler and Mussolini and with their pride on the somber day of defeat. He believes that in time, when they recover their sense of belonging, they, too, will be unwilling to sacrifice their own peculiar consciousness of self to an armada of planetary abstractions. Culture is also refusal. In short, the Resistance is not over; it will soon gain the rest of Europe.

What are the objectives of France? How does she envision the role of European culture tomorrow? The answer is unambiguous. Europe will never renounce its century-old mission. It preserves, undaunted by events, the ambition to serve as the intellectual and spiritual leader of the world, as a conqueror whose aim remains the freedom of the individual. Europe's great diversity of national traditions ever streaming through porous frontiers, its central position between the Russia it enlightened and the Americas it populated and civilized, its long experience of the world and of man, give it even today a privileged position, a position it must defend at all costs.

After all, the technical civilization that is sweeping the world was originally European; but in Europe that civilization flourished in a specific religious, artistic, and scientific context. Today those techniques are avidly imitated and servilely adopted by every new nation, but ordinarily without the accompanying intellectual and spiritual counterbalance that gave an excuse, a purpose, and a personality to the mastery of matter. Europe is bound by duty to express forcefully to the new nations and to repeat untiringly to itself that technical prowess is not the essential objective. At most it is a consequence, although a dangerously alluring one. Separated from its cultural origins, from tradition and restraint, it is bad, almost deadly. For what use is affluence if there is nothing left in man to be enriched?

Eventually Europe will tell the new nations what De Gaulle just told Iran: Preserve your independence, seek out that degree of solitude necessary to your self-discovery; do not surrender your nascent modern being, your personality still undefined, to the bored, impersonal appetites of political giants who, driven by the monstrous necessities of size and security, roam the steppes of a divided world. Jealously consolidate yourself before entering into vast alliances. Look at Europe, which is not through being born; the synthesis of Athens, Rome, and Jerusalem that slowly formed Europe is still incomplete, still in the process of becoming. And we Europeans will help you, since we are not so affluent that we cannot understand the dignity of want or remember the meaning of poverty.

Will such a language be heard, will it prove effective? Probably; so long as Europe itself does not succumb to the sweet appeals of excessive comfort and to the oppression of abundance. For today, in a paradoxical yet incontestable manner, Russia attracts the masses of destitute nations in the very degree that she has failed to reach her vaunted goals of economic prosperity, while the United States, due to her very material success, remains more or less unattractive and her example often spurned. In the eyes of the underdeveloped countries the United States is too remote. She is no longer capable of understanding poverty, excessively bent on eliminating it as some sort of shameful sin, instead of accepting, elevating, and infusing it with a significance that every faith recognizes in denial and want.

Such is not the case with Europe. Yet to speak in a persuasive manner to the underdeveloped countries Europe must make an enormous investment in education, a balanced education, both technical and humanistic. And in fact the greatest single problem facing France is education. This seems strange in a nation whose excellence in this field is universally recognized. Where else is secondary schoolteaching so thorough, where else is it ministered by well-known scholars and thinkers, where else are standards as high? This is precisely the question. Standards are too awesome, they do not provide for the average student. Furthermore, the insistence on humanistic studies and on theoretical science has deprived France of engineers and technicians. Even the best students from Africa and Asia have been unable to meet the stiff requirements for admission to advanced work. As a result, France in recent years had been losing her influence abroad and creating discontents at home.

She has now set about remedying the situation. Technical lycées have been opened, specialized institutes in the applied sciences established, and an ever increasing percentage of the national budget (17 per cent in 1963) is being devoted to education. This is only the beginning since both the press and public opinion are clamoring for a greater effort. Circumstances have been complicated by a remarkable rise in the birth rate. Rapidly progressing on a demographic surge, France, tottering a generation ago as the oldest population in the world, has become one of the most youthful. Whether babies are the product of the new spirit, or whether the country has found hope and confidence in the solace afforded in numbers, it remains that the demographic factor is compelling the government to a drastic and imaginative overhaul of education.

Henceforth, children at about the age of twelve are directed, on the basis of performance and aptitude, either toward the classical or the technical lycée. Many parents find it difficult to approve of the new curriculum, and swallow hard on learning that their children are condemned to lucrative careers as engineers or chemists instead of being allowed to starve nobly on the rhetoric of Vergil and Racine. In accordance with the program of reform, old universities have been resurrected and enlarged, new ones built both in France and in Africa. The Centre National de la Recherche Scientifique offers innumerable opportunities for subsidized research in every field of intellectual pursuit, and an Under-Secretariat of Research has been created to co-ordinate and promote all phases of scientific investigation. The Ministry of Cultural Affairs is active in the areas of the social sciences, pure science, the arts, and the humanities, while the French Cultural Services, dependent on the Quai d'Orsay and to a lesser extent on the Ministry of Education, are supported in their work abroad by funds which put to shame every other nation except Russia. French schools and universities overseas are now holding their own and even expanding, bolstered by numerous parochial schools and by the proverbial zeal of missionaries who tend naturally enough to associate the Gospel with French culture. In Algeria alone, despite troubled conditions, some twelve thousand French teachers are responsible for half of the formal education afforded by the new state.

Such vast undertakings undoubtedly will have to be extended and accelerated if France is to regain her former stature. This leads to a question of primary importance, the hardest for this age to solve intelligently, charitably: that of the survival of languages, the struggle in mortal combat of one language against another, and the inevitable linguistic imperialism which every ambitious nation practices. The French are particularly sensitive on this point, not only because they are convinced of the suppleness, clarity, and durability of the French idiom, but also because the deepest spiritual need of man is neither justice nor order, but meaning. After all, peoples, poets, and philosophers are only as intelligent as the language they speak. It is a person's language that thinks for him.

It would be nice to hope that the extension of language instruction throughout the world will thwart the impending linguistic animosity. In the meantime, however, language, the source and conveyor of culture, is a political weapon, an instrument of domination. In this regard, the noticeable resurgence of French and its eventual consolidation in Europe, the very promotion of the French influence in the European Community, will depend in large part on the continued presence and persistent increase of the French idiom in Africa and in the Maghreb. To the extent that French becomes the literate tongue of West Africa, it will prosper in Europe.

Here again the tie with technology is evident. Unless France regains her century-old technical brilliance, and there are indications that she will, her idiom will wane and wither. Paradoxically enough, for a few more decades, the languages of technology will be the dynamic languages.

From that point of view, the growing influence of Teilhard de Chardin may play a determining role. His followers hail the mystic thought of this distinguished paleontologist and geologist as the

17

most compelling philosophy since Hegel and Marx. Because it expounds the ideal that God above is God ahead, Marxists and Christians have found it to be the only modern philosophy which could bring them together. And no doubt, the fact that Teilhard, a Jesuit, has been the object of a papal *Monitum* against his works makes him quite attractive in many quarters. Throughout Africa, Teilhard seminars are being conducted, some of them organized and attended by chiefs of state. There are many echoes in Teilhard reminiscent of the pilgrims of the absolute: the depiction of the whole universe as sacramental, the belief that there is no such thing as Matter and Spirit but only Matter becoming Spirit, the conviction that the Mystical Body is a biological totality which, through the activity of mankind, will encompass the universe. Not only does Teilhard's passionate vision of the earth appeal to the sensuous and religious temperament of Africans, but it also brings them a rational, optimistic, and systematic interpretation of the future. In Teilhard's eyes, the next step in human evolution is not a further association of cells creating a more complex and heavy brain structure, but the emergence of a single psychic and spiritual center. Work, technology, and faith are to effect a total scientific and social synthesis, a universal regrouping of mankind at a point called Omega where fusion with God will be possible. This so long as humanity has preserved and fostered a development of the personality. Whatever the consequence of Teilhard's thought, it must be considered as symbolic of the new France, attentive both to technology and spiritual values. There is even a parallel between De Gaulle and Teilhard; for in the latter's burning message, technology and poetry are reconciled, progress and faith exalted.

France will be walking a tightrope in the next decade, seeking to develop rapidly in the technical areas while preserving her vocation for art, literature, and the theoretical sciences. To accomplish this, a measure of solitude and rebellious independence is necessary. As Lewis Mumford puts it, "Life cannot be delegated."

St. Bernard, St. Louis, Joan of Arc, even Gambetta and Clemenceau were all solitary rebels. Their message, their acts, were pure folly, senseless risk. The nation followed them grudgingly at times, but follow them it did, only to abandon them to a death of absolute loneliness. Nevertheless, it is they who are France, any Frenchman knows it instinctively.

France is not wary of her friends, but of herself and of that somewhat tired, rasping old voice of wisdom that says: "Be reasonable, be cautious, play it safe, enjoy your wines, the laugh of your children and Atlantic bliss." Yet France is only herself when utterly youthful, rebellious, and risking.

If one can speak for France in this conclusion, it is to plead in favor of a contradiction that can help preserve Europe and the world's complexity. A belligerent message? Perhaps; but what else are the endless chorales of beauty and truth that haunt men's lives if not the voice of hope singing an infinite fugue of refusal?

---

1. In reality Mauriac, a spirited admirer of De Gaulle, rarely sees him. This in order to be more convincing in his support of the president, in order not to be accused of subordinating his political opinions to the demands of a personal friendship. Yet there can be no doubt that Mauriac and De Gaulle are very close indeed.

The Legal Structure of the European Community   CARL H. FULDA

THE TREATY OF ROME, which created the European Economic Community, is not the only instrument of European unification,[1] but it is by far the most important one. Negotiated in 1957, and effective since January 1, 1958, it includes the "Six" (Belgium, France, Germany, Holland, Italy, and Luxembourg) as full members, and Greece and Turkey,[2] and eighteen African states[3] as associate members. An assignment to survey the numerous provisions of this Treaty and the many Regulations and Decisions promulgated thereunder is both precarious and challenging: precarious because a legal summary may be viewed with apprehension of dullness as part of a collection of essays by distinguished historians, political scientists, and economists, and challenging since it presents an opportunity to demonstrate that lawyers are the architects of institutions which translate ideas of social progress into living realities.

The Treaty has been called a "framework-law." It contains many broad policy directives which are not self-executing, but require implementation by the institutions of the Community and by the member states. Its basic program is to bring about a fusion of the separate economies of the member states into one single integrated market which will promote "a harmonious development of economic activities, a continuous and balanced expansion, increased stability and an accelerated standard of living. . . . "[4] This Common Market is being established in accordance with a timetable calling for a transitional period divided into three stages. The first stage was declared terminated at the end of 1961,[5] and this has been hailed as an event marking the point of no return, because Article 8 of the Treaty, anticipating difficulties which did not materialize, provided for elaborate proceedings for extension of the first stage culminating in arbitration if no agreement on transition to the second stage could be reached after the first four years. By contrast, further progress will be almost automatic because the second and third stages of four years each may not be extended or curtailed except pursuant to a unanimous decision by the Council on a proposal of the Commission.[6] Accordingly, the end of the transitional period may be expected to be reached on January 1, 1970.

It is essential to keep this timetable in mind in order to appraise fairly the record of the Community during the first six years of its existence. Moreover, the Community is a rather loose-knit organization in comparison with the United States. It has no federal government, no common currency, no common foreign policy, and the legal systems of its member states vary widely in administrative practices, tax structures, subsidies, and other important matters. Nevertheless, the Community is a "legal personality"[7] which pursues economic rather than political union.

THE PROGRAM OF ECONOMIC INTEGRATION

The governing principle of economic integration is to be found in Article 7 which states that

> within the field of application of this Treaty, and without prejudice to any particular provisions mentioned therein, any discrimination on the ground of nationality shall be prohibited.

The rule that each member state must treat the nationals of other member states in the same manner as it treats its own nationals is a constitutional norm of the Community which is designed to erase boundaries, just as the interstate-commerce, privileges and immunities, and supremacy clauses of the American Constitution accomplished legal unification of the United States.[8] From this norm follow four basic freedoms, each of which must be examined in some detail.

The Free Movement of Goods

There shall be no discrimination against goods on the basis of their origin or destination within the Community. In other words, the Community shall become a customs union: tariffs and quota restrictions shall be abolished in the trade between the member states, and there shall be only a common external tariff which shall reflect the average of the tariffs of the member states.[9] Consequently, high tariffs levied by some member states on goods coming into the Community from third countries will be reduced, and low tariffs levied by other member states will be raised.

Obviously, the customs union could not be built up without imposing on the member states a "stand still" obligation: there shall be no new customs duties or quantitative restrictions in intra-community trade.[10]

The Customs Union is to date (November, 1963) the most advanced part of the Common Market program. Internal tariffs on industrial products have been reduced by 60 per cent since January 1, 1958, and on some agriculture products by 40 per cent.[11] The significance of these reductions of industrial tariffs is apparent from a reading of Article 14, paragraph 6, of the Treaty, which obligates the member states to "endeavor to ensure that the reduction applied to the duties on each product shall amount: . . . at the end of the the second stage, to at least 50 per cent of the basic duty." The end of the second stage will occur on December 31, 1965.

The establishment of the Common External Tariff is also ahead of schedule.[12] Indeed, the great impact of the Community on the outside world is attributable, in large measure, to the existence of that tariff, and to the authority of the Commission to negotiate on behalf of the Community with third countries with respect to that tariff[13] and other commercial matters.[14] It was this authority for across-the-board tariff negotiations which persuaded the American Congress to grant similar authority to the President of the United

States in the Trade Expansion Act of 1962 in order to enable him to bargain effectively with the European Community.[15] Such bargaining will begin in Geneva in 1964—the so-called Kennedy Round. The principal difficulty is presented by the fact that a large list of products bears United States duties of more than 25 per cent, while there are only seven such items in the Common External Tariff.[16] Hence, a slash of 10 per cent of the latter would result in a duty much lower than a similar reduction of the former.

It should be added that the Common External Tariff causes some difficulties even for the member states. Germany, for example, repeatedly requested relief from hardship claimed to have been caused by the Common Tariff. In one case, that tariff had raised Germany's duties on wine imported from third countries, and the Government of the Federal Republic petitioned the Commission in Brussels for relief pursuant to Article 25 of the Treaty. It desired the establishment of a "tariff quota," a specified quantity which may be imported at reduced rates or duty free from outside the Community. The Commission granted the request in part only, but the European Court of Justice annulled the partial denial on the ground that the Commission's order was vague and contradictory, and, therefore, not supported by reasons as required by Article 190 of the Treaty.[17] In a similar case the Court dismissed on the merits Germany's complaint against a decision of the Commission which had refused a request for suspension of the common tariff on oranges;[18] this judicial affirmation of the Commission's power to deny the relief demanded by a member state shows that, with respect to the subject matter here involved, the Court acted like a Federal Supreme Court for the Community. Significantly, nine of the thirteen decisions of the Court interpreting the Treaty of Rome which had been handed down by the end of October, 1963, involved disputes concerning tariffs.

The Free Movement of Persons

The second freedom, which follows from the principle of non-discrimination, is the freedom of workers and of business firms to move within the Community. With respect to workers, this has been facilitated by severe labor shortages in many places, which forced importation of foreigners, particularly from southern Italy. Nevertheless, the provisions of the Treaty have been implemented by Regulation 15 of the Council[19] which authorizes any national of a member state "to hold gainful employment in the territory of another Member State" if no appropriate candidate for the unfilled position has been found within a period of three weeks after the vacancy has been registered at the labor bureau. The Regulation contains many details as to extension of employment, equality of treatment, the worker's family, social-security benefits, and administrative collaboration among member states. Most significantly, it ordains that

> the legislative, regulatory and administrative provisions which set a limit, in a Member State, to the number or to the percentage of foreign workers employed, by enterprise, by field of occupation, by region, or on a national scale are not applicable to workers who are nationals of other Member States.

Here is supranational, or "federal," legislation superseding state laws.

The corollary right of individuals and firms to engage in activities other than earning of wages is called the Right of Establishment,[20] which is guaranteed for the benefit of nationals of member states and companies set up in conformity with the laws of a member state whose registered office, central administration, or principal place of business is located within the Community. The Council of Ministers issued on December 18, 1961, a "General Program for the Abolition of Restrictions on Freedom of Establishment"[21] which contains a detailed time-table by groups of industries. The program enumerates explicitly a number of restrictive provisions and practices with regard to foreigners only which must be eliminated.[22] This program requires harmonization of the internal laws of the member states not only in the described particulars, but also in related matters. For instance, provisions in national corporation laws which prohibit transfer of the corporate seat to other countries would be incompatible with the Treaty in so far as intra-Community transfers are concerned.[23] The general program was issued pursuant to Article 54 of the Treaty. Compliance is an obligation of the member states.

The Freedom to Render Services

The third freedom is the freedom to render services everywhere in the Community (Art. 59). This freedom applies to the extent that the services involved are not covered by any one of the other freedoms. For instance, a French insurance company could establish a branch office in Germany by virtue of the right of establishment; it could sell insurance in Germany without being established there on the basis of the right to render services. Here again, a general program was issued by the Council,[24] which includes the announcement of an examination "as to whether the lifting of restrictions on the free provision of services should be preceded, accompanied, or followed by the mutual recognition of diplomas, certificates and other evidences of qualification, as well as by the co-ordination of the legislative, regulatory or administrative provisions regarding these services."

The Free Movement of Capital

Restrictions on movement of capital belonging to persons resident in the member states must be abolished in accordance with a Directive of the Council.[25]

THE POLICY TO CARRY OUT THE PROGRAM OF INTEGRATION

The "Rules Governing Competition"[26] are an essential instrument to bring about economic integration. Without them, the Customs Union would be meaningless because the removal of tariffs and quota restrictions could be nullified by cartels which would erect private restrictions against the free movement of goods. In other words, the borders between the member states should be erased in so far as economic activities are concerned, and this requires prohibition of all obstacles to trade, be they of governmental or private origin. Accordingly, Article 92 declares that subsidies granted by a member state which distort or threaten to distort competition by favoring certain enterprises shall be incompatible with the Common Market *"to the extent to which it adversely affects trade between Member States."* Similarly, Article 85 prohibits

all agreements between enterprises, all decisions by associations of enterprises and all concerted practices *which are liable to affect trade between member states* and which are designed to prevent, restrict or distort cometition within the Common Market or which have this effect. Thisp shall, in particular, include:

  (a) the direct or indirect fixing of purchase or selling prices or of any other trading conditions;

  (b) the limitation or control of production, markets, technical development or investment;

  (c) market-sharing or the sharing of sources of supply;

  (d) the application of unequal conditions to parties undertaking equivalent engagements in commercial transactions, thereby placing them at a competitive disadvantage;

  (e) making the conclusion of a contract subject to the acceptance by the other party to the contract of additional obligations, which, by their nature or according to commercial practice, have no connection with the subject of such contract. (Italics added.)

The crucial clause in this European equivalent of Section 1 of the American Sherman Antitrust Act is the requirement that trade among the member states must be affected by the agreement. This clause defines the coverage and the jurisdictional limits of the law governing the Community as distinguished from the law of each one of the member states,[27] and it is this co-existence of Community law and national laws in the same territory which reflects the federalist nature of the Community. Indeed, the condition as to the likely effect on trade between the member states is comparable to the interstate commerce clause in the Sherman Act and in the United States Constitution; American federal economic legislation is applicable only to interstate transactions, just as Article 85 of the Treaty of Rome governs only those agreements whose scope and effect transcend the boundaries of one member state.

It is impossible to predict whether the interpretation of this European version of "interstate commerce" will become as broad as in the United States.[28] For the time being, however, it is likely that the enforcement activities of the Commission and much litigation in the national courts will involve agreements between parties resident in different member states. Typical examples are contracts between manufacturer X in one member state and dealer Y in another pursuant to which the latter assumes an exclusive distributorship in his country for the products of the former. The effect of the monopoly of distribution granted to Y on trade between member states is obvious.

Pursuant to Article 87 of the Treaty, the Council issued Regulation 17, which became effective on March 13, 1962.[29] Its basic feature is a notification procedure which generally requires submission to the Commission in Brussels of agreements falling under the prohibition of Article 85; accordingly almost a thousand cartel agreements and close to thirty-five thousand bilateral agreements (mainly involving vertical arrangements between manufacturers and distributors, and patentees and their licensees) which were in effect on March 13, 1962, have been filed. The Commission must be notified of new agreements forthwith after they have been entered into. The purpose of this procedure is twofold: In the first place, it gives to the Commission access to facts which it otherwise may not be able to discover in view of its limited investigatory powers. Secondly, the notification is an indispensable prerequisite for obtaining a declaration from the Commission that the agreement is valid pursuant to the third paragraph of Article 85. That paragraph permits legalization of agreements which "improve the production or distribution of goods, or . . . promote technical or economic progress, while allowing consumers a fair share of the resulting profit"; in addition, the agreement must not involve restrictions greater than those needed to attain these objectives, and it must not eliminate competition with respect to a substantial part of the goods concerned. An American antitrust lawyer would call this a statutory "rule of reason": it authorizes agreements with demonstrable benefits for producers and consumers which outweigh relatively minor restrictions on competition.

The full impact of Article 85 will become apparent only after the Commission has rendered a number of decisions with respect to the agreements filed with it. Such decisions may be expected in 1964 and 1965. In the meantime, a Regulation outlining the hearing procedure governing such cases was published in the *Official Journal* of the Community on August 20, 1963.[30] The Commission may require that firms and individuals cease and desist from infringing the Rules of the Treaty and may impose fines for violations of its orders,[31] subject, of course, to judicial review by the Court of Justice of the Community.

Regulation 17 has made possible systematic and uniform enforcement of the antitrust rules by the Commission, and it is most significant that the Commission has sole and exclusive jurisdiction to declare whether or not the "rule of reason" of Article 85(3) is applicable in any particular case. Nevertheless, the national authorities of the member states retain the power to prosecute violations of the Treaty Rules[32] as long as the Commission has not initiated proceedings. Liaison with the authorities of the member states is carried on, primarily, through a Consultative Committee on Cartels and Monopolies.

It may be added that in October, 1963, roughly six years after the Treaty took effect and nineteen months after Regulation 17 came into force, the Commission had issued a confidential recommendation to an important cartel; in the event of refusal to comply, this would become the first major case for litigation. In the United States, it took more than ten years after enactment of the Sherman Act to start meaningful enforcement.

THE INSTITUTIONS OF THE COMMUNITY

One can readily see, from the examples discussed, the Treaty requires implementation by Regulations and Directives to the member governments. In short, Community law must be legislated either directly by the Community, or by the member states following Community instructions. This legislative power is vested, not in the European Parliament,[33] which has only advisory functions, but in the Council of Ministers,[34] in which each member government is represented by one member. The Community is thus exposed to the strains and stresses of conflicting political interests and pressures. This weakness is, however, mitigated to a considerable extent by the requirement that on most major matters the Council shall act only on a proposal of the Commission, which it may amend only by unanimous vote. The Commission consists of nine individuals who "shall perform their duties in the general interest of the Community with complete independence" and "shall not seek or accept instructions from any Government or other body."[35]

The voting in the Council is based on the theory that the larger members should have greater voting strength than the smaller ones. Hence, Germany, France, and Italy each have four votes; Belgium and Holland, each two votes; and Luxembourg, one vote.[36] During the first stage of the transitional period unanimity was required for practically all votes; during the current second stage, a qualified majority of twelve votes is sufficient in some instances, and during the third and last stage a qualified majority becomes the rule.[37] This indicates again the importance of the declaration, cited above, that the second stage began on January 1, 1962.

The responsibilities of the Commission, apart from its power to make recommendations to the Council, are, as has been explained, executive or administrative. It may make decisions in many cases specified in the Treaty.[38] For instance, it is authorized to dispose of applications by member states for temporary relief from their obligations arising under the Treaty provisions relating to abolition of tariffs and quotas in intra-Community trade.

The ultimate arbiter of the Community law is, of course, the Court of Justice, composed of seven judges who sit in Luxembourg.[39] Its jurisdiction extends to four principal categories of cases:

1. An individual may challenge a decision by the Commission;
2. A member state may challenge the lawfulness of an act of the Council or Commission;
3. In a suit brought in a national court which involves interpretation of the Treaty or of acts of the Council or Commission, the national court may, and, if it is a court of last

resort, must refer such questions to the Community court; and

4. The Commission may sue any member state which, in its opinion, has violated the Treaty. Similarly, any member state may sue any other member state for the same reason.

A few examples illustrating the third and fourth group may be helpful to complete the picture.

1. Dutch importers protested tariff assessments made against them by the Dutch Customs Administration. They contended that the reclassification of certain German goods, for tariff purposes, had resulted in a higher import duty than that applied at the time the Treaty came into force, in violation of Article 12 which obligates the member states to refrain from introducing, as among themselves, any new customs duties or charges with equivalent effect and from increasing such duties or charges. The Dutch government argued that Article 12 gave no right to an individual importer to complain about the tariff imposed by his own government. The Dutch Tariff Commission referred the question to the European Court, which sustained the importer's position, holding that Article 12 did vest individual rights in the citizens of the Community which national courts (including national administrative courts such as the Tariff Commission) must safeguard. The Court remanded the case to the Dutch authorities for ascertainment whether the assessment on the plaintiff exceeded the duties actually applied at the time the Treaty became effective, adding that an increase could result either from a change of rate or a change of classification.[40]

This decision is most significant. The view rejected by the Court, that only governments could vindicate compliance with Article 12, reflected traditional concepts of public international law in interpreting treaties between sovereign states. The contrary holding indicates that the Treaty of Rome may be likened to a Constitution, which creates rights based on "federal" law.[41]

Referral of questions involving the Treaty law has also occurred in disputes involving the rules of competition. Indeed, it is likely to be used frequently in that area. One recent example is a claim for damages by the exclusive French distributor of a German product against a French competitor who somehow had obtained the same German goods and had sold them in France. The Commerce Court in Paris decided in favor of the plaintiff, but the Court of Appeals suspended the proceedings pending a decision by the Commission in Brussels and the European Court on the question whether the plaintiff's exclusive contract could be justified under the "rule of reason" of Article 85, paragraph 3, of the Treaty.[42]

2. Perhaps the most dramatic manifestation of the Community may be found in the decisions in which the Court sustained complaints by the Commission that a member state had violated its obligations under the Treaty. The very first case that occurred under the Treaty of Rome involved that issue.[43] The Italian government had temporarily suspended all imports of pork, in order to eliminate a glut on the market. It had failed to apply for relief pursuant to Article 226, which permits the Commission, during the transitional period, to authorize emergency measures of safeguard against economic dislocations. The Court held that Italy had violated Article 31 of the Treaty, which forbids member states from adding new restrictions to intra-Community trade, and that Italy could not take the law into its own hands by ignoring the escape-clause procedure provided by the Treaty.

Significantly, the Treaty provides no enforcement machinery for such judgments against member states. It proceeds on the theory that compliance with such judgments will be a matter of course, and that a contrary action would mean the destruction of the Community. Presumably, the continuation of the Community and retention of membership in it is immensely more important than the receipt of a favorable judgment by a defendant in such a case.

CONCLUSION

Much American public reaction to the Common Market seems to have gone from one extreme to the other. Initial enthusiasm greeted the Community as the long awaited United States of Europe, an oversentimentalized exaggeration which, after the French veto of

British membership in January, 1963, gave way to funeral orations which probably reflected a similarly unrealistic appraisal. To be sure, the historic experiment is not yet out of the woods. Its greatest peril arises from the difficulties of establishing a common agricultural policy, a subject treated elsewhere in this volume. In addition, the Community's commercial relationship with the outside world is still a matter of speculation. Much depends on the success or failure of the tariff negotiations in Geneva in 1964. But without minimizing these caveats, the Community represents an enormous and unprecedented step forward, potentially the most promising in the Western world since the founding of the United States of America.

Anyone who denies this should compare the Europe of today with the Europe of the 1930's. The standard of living is higher than it ever was, with the possible exception of that of southern Italy. Currencies are freely convertible, and labor shortages exist in most places. The work of harmonizing and unifying the legal systems of the various countries is progressing; for instance, a European patent may soon be available, thus obviating the necessity of registering a patent in each country.[44] The assertion that this change of climate would have come about without the Community is utterly lacking in plausibility.

Imagine a prophet who had predicted in 1933, the year of Hitler's accession to power, that less than thirty years later a court composed of seven judges representing six nationalities could tell a sovereign government to mend its ways and not only get away with it but obtain instantaneous compliance. Such a prophet would, perhaps, have been locked up in an insane asylum; more likely, he would have been shot for treason.

It may be argued that all this is fine but that without political unity it does not amount to much. Perhaps the absence of political unity will eventually spell the doom of the uncompleted experiment. But it need not turn out that way. Possibly, future historians may hail the authors of the Treaty of Rome for having perceived that economic unification must come first, and that only if it succeeds, will the rest follow as a matter of course. The present Community, which at midpoint of its transitional period has been compared to a promising teenager, is a loose-knit federalistic structure. More than that cannot be expected from a population approximately as large as that of the United States, which speaks four different languages and looks back upon two thousand years of differing histories and cultures marked with recurring clashes of bloody conflicts.

1. Others are the European Free Trade Association (EFTA), which binds its members (Austria, Denmark, Norway, Portugal, Sweden, Switzerland, and the United Kingdom) to reduce and ultimately eliminate tariffs (*United Nations Treaty Series*, Vol. CCCLXX [1960], p. 5; the European Coal and Steel Community [1952]; and the European Atomic Energy Community [1957]).

2. The Convention with Greece, signed on July 9, 1961, was ratified on August 24, 1962, and became effective on November 1, 1962 (Commerce Clearing House, *Common Market Reports* [1962], #9014 [hereinafter cited as *CMR*]). The parties pledge to abolish all discrimination based on nationality and to form a customs union. A similar agreement with Turkey was initialed on June 25, 1962, and is at the date of writing (November, 1963) awaiting ratification (*CMR*, #9065, #9088).

3. A new convention was signed July 20, 1963, pursuant to the authority of Article 136 of the Treaty. See *CMR*, #5981, for a summary of its provisions.

4. Art. 2.

5. Proclamation by the Council of Ministers of January 14, 1962 (*Official Journal*, 164/62).

6. Art. 8(5).

7. Art. 210.

8. Art. I, sec. 8 (clause 2), gives Congress the power "to regulate Commerce with foreign nations, and among the several states . . . "; Art. IV, sec. 2, provides that "the citizens of each State shall be entitled to all Privileges and Immunities of Citizens in the several States." According to Art. VI, "the Constitution, and the laws of the United States which shall be made in Pursuance thereof . . . shall be the Supreme law of the land. . . . "

9. Art. 19.

10. Arts. 12 and 31.

11. *CMR*, #9081.

12. *Ibid.*

13. Arts. 111(2), 113, and 114. During the transitional period, the member states shall co-ordinate their commercial relations with third countries in accordance with the Council's decisions published in the *Official Journal* of November 4, 1961.

14. The first commercial agreement between the Community and a third country—Iran—was initialed on September 25, 1963. *CMR*, #9087.

15. The Act (19 U.S.C.A. § 1801 *et seq.*) authorizes the President to increase or decrease tariffs by 50 per cent. The additional authority to

eliminate all tariffs on goods with respect to which the United States and the European Economic Community together account for 80 per cent or more of the aggregated world export value was based on the assumption of British entry into the Community and is without practical value at this time.

16. Pierre Uri, *Partnership for Progress: A Program for Transatlantic Action* (New York and Evanston, 1963), pp. 122, 123.

17. *Government of the Federal Republic of Germany* v. *Commission of the European Economic Community,* Case No. 24/62, decided July 4, 1963, *CMR,* #8012.

18. *Government of the Federal Republic of Germany* v. *Commission of the European Economic Community,* Case No. 34/62, July 15, 1963, *CMR,* #8016.

19. Published in the *Official Journal* on August 26, 1961; *CMR,* #1031. A new Regulation No. 38/64 took effect on May 1, 1964, published in the *Official Journal,* April 17, 1964.

20. Part 2, Title III, chap. 2 of the Treaty (Arts. 52–58).

21. Published in the *Official Journal* of January 15, 1962; *CMR,* #1351.

22. Among them are: prohibitions of access to or exercise of non-wage earning activities; condition of such access on foreigner's authorizations; barring or limiting membership in companies; limitations of the right to enter into contracts, to acquire and exploit property, to borrow money, to sue and be sued. See also Articles 220 and 221 of the Treaty, imposing additional duties on the member states to insure equality of treatment to nationals of all members states.

23. Peter Hay, "Four Lectures on the Common Market: Trade Provisions— German and French Company Law—Establishment," *University of Pittsburgh Law Review,* XXIV (1963), 754 ff.

24. *Official Journal,* January 15, 1962; *CMR,* #1521; Art. 63 of the Treaty.

25. *Official Journal,* July 12, 1960, and January 22, 1963; *CMR,* #1651. Arts. 67–73 of the Treaty.

26. Part 3, Title I, chap. 1 of the Treaty (Arts. 85–94). Article 3(f) lists the establishment of a system insuring that competition will not be distorted in the Common Market as one of the activities of the Community.

27. All of the member states except Italy and Luxembourg have enacted national antitrust laws. The German law is the most elaborate. See Loftus Becker, "The Antitrust Laws of the Common Market," *American Bar Association Antitrust Section Reports,* XVII (1960), 456; Grant Kelleher, "The National Antitrust Laws of Europe," *ibid.,* p. 506.

28. See Carl H. Fulda, "Antitrust in the European Economic Community," *Texas Law Review,* XLI (1963), 394–97.

29. *CMR,* #2401.

30. *CMR,* #2635.

31. These fines would be collected by the national authorities of the member states pursuant to Article 192 of the Treaty.

32. Including Article 86 which prohibits abuse of market-dominating positions.

33. See Arts. 137–44. The deputies are members of the legislative assemblies of the member states. Their power to vote the Commission out of office has not so far been exercised.

34. Arts. 145–54.

35. Art. 157.

36. Art. 148.

37. For details see Ernst Wohlfarth, Ulrich Everling, Hans Joachim Glaesner, and Rudolf Sprung, *Die Europäische Wirtschaftsgemeinschaft: Kommentar zum Vertrag* (Berlin and Frankfort, 1960), pp. 447 ff.

38. See the list in Wohlfarth *et al., op. cit.,* p. 461.

39. Arts. 164–88.

40. *N.V. Algemene Transport—en Expeditie Onderneming Van Gend & Loos* v. *Netherlands Fiscal Administration,* Case No. 26/62, February 5, 1963, *CMR,* #8008; *Da Costa en Schaake N.V., Amsterdam, Jacob Meijer N.V., Venlo and Hoechst—Holland N.V., Amsterdam* v. *Netherlands Fiscal Administration,* Cases No. 28/62, 29/62, and 30/62, March 27, 1963, *CMR,* #8010.

41. See Peter Hay, "Federal Jurisdiction of the Common Market Court," *American Journal of Comparative Law,* XII (1963), 21.

42. *Société Union Nationale des Economies Familiales* v. *Etablissements Consten, CMR,* #8009.

43. *Commission* v. *Italy,* Case No. 7/61, December 19, 1961; *CMR,* #8001.

44. Draft Convention Relating to European Patent Law, *CMR,* 3471.

France and European Security
KLAUS KNORR

ON JANUARY 14, 1963, General de Gaulle greatly shocked Europe and the United States by his sudden and brusque rejection of British entry into the European Economic Community. A few months later, Raymond Aron conceded in *Le Figaro:* "Within NATO French political and military participation has been reduced to a bare minimum. General de Gaulle being, once and for all, against formulas for integration and little inclined to compromise, the compatibility between Gaullist diplomacy and the operation of the European Community or NATO remains in question."[1]

Indeed, the present challenge to NATO and its procedure is fundamental. It is unlike the several disagreements and squabbles that have marked the history of the alliance heretofore. It involves a clash of basic concepts of how Europe and the entire North Atlantic West—highly industrialized, predominantly rich, emphasizing personal freedom in political and economic life—should be organized for its military security and for conducting its relations with the dynamic and forcefully pushing world at large.

In order to understand the full complexity of the problem, one must begin with the familiar fact that western Europe—historically the cradle of powerful nation-states—contained on the eve of World War II four of the seven Great Powers extant, not counting Russia, and ruled the vast bulk of the colonial world, controlling nearly all of Africa and large parts of Asia. By the early 1960's, nearly all of Europe's far-flung colonies had gained their independence; and, although France, Italy, and finally West Germany had rebuilt their military forces, and Britain had become a nuclear power and France was on the way to becoming one, it was fairly clear that, by itself, no west European country could hope to aspire to a status equaling that of the two superpowers. To be sure, the bipolar pattern of world power is giving way to an international system in which effective power is distributed less unevenly than during the 1950's, and more than two major centers of power may come into being eventually; but it is improbable that any one west European nation will become more than a power of middle rank. The arms race, and especially the race in advancing military technology, demands a huge resource base. The simple fact is that both the Soviet Union and the United States exceed in terms of population and economic resources any one west European country by a factor of at least three or four.

Of course, sheer size of territory, population, and economic-productive capacity do not necessarily measure international power. There are forms of international influence that do not rest on numbers or on military and industrial capabilities. But as long as national power is the most potent form of power in the world, as long as military strength remains the ultimate or, at any rate, the indispensable basis of this power, as long as the Soviet Union and the United States do not withdraw from international politics, and as long as their governments command and effectively organize the national resources required for active international engagement— as long as these several conditions prevail, the highly industrialized countries of continental size will, in terms of international power, outrank such smaller nations as France, Great Britain, and Germany.

For the last eighteen years, the military security of western Europe has remained crucially dependent on the United States. Without the United States all the countries of western Europe together did not and do not now dispose of military forces that are remotely a match for the Soviet Union. The divisions of European armies are in number, firepower, and mobility outclassed by the Soviet divisions; and even though Great Britain has nuclear bombs and a fleet of bombers for their delivery, her capability to deter the U.S.S.R. on the nuclear level is, by itself, something less than awe-inspiring.

This decisive military dependence of western Europe on the United States was no doubt inevitable during the first five or ten postwar years while the area recovered from wartime damage. But why has it persisted since? World opinion has become so used to this condition of European dependence that mentioning this relationship is unlikely to cause astonishment. Yet it is a question worth raising. Is it not extraordinary that a group of countries that exceed the Soviet Union and the United States in population, that are highly industrialized, wealthy, scientifically and technologically sophisticated, that face a military superpower of known ruthlessness and possessing world-revolutionary designs—is it not extraordinary that such a group of nations should remain content to derive their security primarily from alliance with another superpower several thousand miles across the sea? In terms of history, this is an amazing fact, and one that calls for explanation.

Of course, although these countries together dispose of enough resources to provide themselves with military capabilities approximating those of the superpowers, the transformation of general resources into military forces would take a great deal of time. It requires years to produce modern divisions and even longer to develop nuclear and other sophisticated weapons systems. What is extraordinary, therefore, is not so much the absence of accomplishment as (with the notable exception of France in recent years) the absence of the attempt.

It is curious that no such attempt has been made. It has been suggested that the populations of western Europe are too engrossed in enjoying their expanding private incomes to regard a larger defense effort, demanding increased taxes and military service, with anything but reluctance. It is also pointed out that, following two murderous wars, Europeans are naturally loath to contemplate seriously preparation for another. And it has been maintained that Europeans are less convinced of military danger emanating from the East than are Americans—though this view is hardly shared in West Germany. All these explanations probably contain some truth.

But one adverse factor has probably been crucial. Though, as clearly observed, these nations possess together the resources for assuring European security, these resources are not subject to one center of decision, and several separate national efforts could hardly hope to make western Europe militarily secure. In terms of producing and deploying military forces, separate national establishments would mean a far less efficient employment of resources than could be achieved through one integrated or at least highly concerted effort; and how much confidence could there be in joint employment of separate forces in the event of aggression by a superpower against a single west European country? Yet, if these objections are granted, why did these nations—six of which at least displayed remarkable creativity in fashioning joint economic institutions—not try to build a solid integrated basis for their joint defense?

One reason has probably been the ready availability of American protection. This explanation has been advanced by General de Gaulle. There is NATO, there are sizable bodies of American troops stationed on the European continent, and there is America's formidable strategic nuclear power. Of course, the European members of NATO have committed forces to Europe's defense, but most of our allies have not made the larger contributions to the Shield which the United States has demanded and to which they have agreed in the councils of NATO. No doubt the alliance has had its inconveniences, and American domination its drawbacks, but to the vast majority of west Europeans NATO seemed a satisfactory security arrangement and, despite recently increasing voices of doubt and dissent, may still be so regarded by most west Europeans. Thus lacking strong incentives, the European nations have not made a determined attempt to push integration on the military level, where it would have encountered powerful resistance, as the French defeat of the project for a European Defense Community indicated.

And yet there is the French challenge today, and there are, outside France, increasing voices of dissatisfaction with NATO as it is, with American domination of NATO, and with complete dependence on American nuclear protection. Four considerations are at the bottom of this dissatisfaction. First, ever since the Soviet Union acquired the nuclear capability to strike at the United States, there have been questions in allied nations about whether the United States could afford to protect, and would in fact protect, western Europe from Soviet aggression by means of a retaliatory threat that might provoke a Soviet first strike against the United States, or that might have to be made good by an American first strike, which would lead to a Soviet retaliatory blow and the destruction of American cities. Stated simply, there have been doubts as to whether or not western Europe can safely rely on the American nuclear umbrella.

Second, many Europeans have been alarmed by the recent shift in American strategy away from primary reliance on the threat of massive nuclear retaliation. The United States now appears to want the West to be capable of a flexible response to any Soviet aggression, including the option of defending Europe by means of conventional forces or, should such a response prove insufficient, through recourse to a limited and selective employment of nuclear weapons, preferably against military rather than civilian targets. This evolution in United States strategic thinking reflects the realization that a reciprocal destruction of cities is suicidal and that its threat therefore lacks credibility; and it furthermore reflects confidence in the superior capability of the United States to wage selective nuclear war, destroying military targets while, for purposes of intra-war deterrence, keeping the threat of city destruction in reserve. In American eyes this posture assures Europeans of protection despite the Soviet ability to bomb American cities. Europeans, however, fear that this strategy increases the danger of a conventional or nuclear war confined to Europe, a war that in either case would destroy much of western Europe's substance. Europeans, by and large, do not want Europe defended by means that are sure to devastate it. They lean toward reliance on strategic nuclear weapons targeted on Soviet cities, and see the chief function of conventional and tactical nuclear forces as precipitating escalation to a level most apt to inspire a would-be aggressor with terror.

Third, there have also been expressions of anxiety over repeated conflicts between the foreign policy of the United States and that of several west European countries. On the one hand, there is some fear that United States responses to communist aggression outside Europe might lead to war and involve Europe although she would have had little or no control over its genesis. And on the other hand, European nations have found on numerous occasions that their own foreign policies lacked American backing or even incurred American disapproval; for example, during numerous crises of decolonization and, dramatically, on the occasion of the Anglo-French Suez venture in 1956. The fiasco that resulted at this time was, perhaps, due not so much to a vague nuclear threat by the U.S.S.R. as to the fact that the American ally, instead of lending support, exerted strong pressure against the action. More recently, the conclusion of the test-ban agreement and the prospect of further arrangements for arms control between Moscow and Washington have stimulated anxiety, particularly in the Federal Republic of Germany, that the United States might sacrifice essentially European interests in her bargaining negotiations with the Soviet Union.

Finally, there is the matter of pride. In view of Europe's great past, many west Europeans find it hard to tolerate overwhelming dependence on the United States. One is accustomed to speak of NATO as a partnership. In fact, it is a coalition of necessarily very unequal partners. The United States possesses, and wants to preserve, a monopoly or quasi-monopoly on the nuclear weapons that, technologically, are the decisive arms in this age. That many Europeans find their roles as protégés of the United States frustrating and demeaning is surely understandable. They fret under their sense of inferior status.

The chief exponent of European dissatisfaction on these counts is, of course, General de Gaulle. At his press conference of July 29, 1963, when he announced the French refusal to accede to the test ban negotiated at Moscow, he did not deny that the Atlantic alliance was an "elementary necessity." But he also stated the reasons why, in his view, France and Europe required independence of action and the military means on which such independence must rest:

> As far as defense is concerned, until recently, thanks to their nuclear armament, the Americans were in a position to assure the free world of

semi-absolute protection. But they have lost this monopoly. . . . The fact that the Russians also now possess enough to destroy the universe, and notably the new continent, makes it natural that America sees her *own* survival as the principal objective of an eventual conflict and envisions the moment and the degree and the methods of her nuclear intervention for the defense of other regions only as a function of that natural and overriding necessity.[2]

De Gaulle also referred to ". . . the separate negotiations between the Anglo-Saxons and the Soviets, which, starting from the restricted nuclear test agreement, appear to be about to be extended to other questions, notably European quesions, and, so far, in the absence of the Europeans. This evidently runs counter to the views of France. . . . For the moment, France would not subscribe to some arrangements that would be carried out above her head and which would concern Europe and notably Germany." And he concluded: "France will not be diverted by the Moscow agreements from equipping herself with the means of immeasurable destruction possessed by the other powers. Failing which, since the others have it, her own security and her own independence would never more belong to her."[3] This, it seems, is the heart of General de Gaulle's position. Whether he refers to France alone or to Europe (from which he excluded England—that other "Anglo-Saxon" country), he sees each as requiring security and each as requiring independence that is not in the main derived from, and hence is virtually dependent on, the power of others, but truly belongs to herself.

The position of De Gaulle is a powerful challenge to NATO and particularly to the United States. It may well imply that, in its present form, NATO will not be viable much longer. According to the views of the Kennedy Administration, there is nothing basically wrong with the NATO structure. To those on the western side of the Atlantic, this structure seems to serve the interests both of the United States and Europe. If only France were to desist from her effort to gain an independent nuclear posture, Britain to give up hers, and America's European allies to prove amenable to a demand for substantially strengthened Shield forces—Washington would be satisfied. Ideally, the United States would like to possess a nuclear monopoly in the alliance and to see the alliance capable of defending western Europe against anything but a premeditated all-out attack by non-strategic, and preferably conventional, forces.

From the strictly military viewpoint, this American position makes a great deal of sense as long as one assumes that the security interests of the United States and western Europe are virtually identical. It aspires to a unitary and hence effective control of nuclear weapons, thus minimizing the chances of a nuclear conflict's being precipitated by inadvertence or irresponsible conduct, and maximizing the prospects of efficient employment in the event of war. The nuclear capability of the United States is at present so strong that the nuclear force any of her allies could manage to acquire on its own would seem to be of little account in the event of general war. Moreover, the more effective nuclear strategy aims to avoid the mutually suicidal mass destruction of cities by considering the option of limiting strategic strikes to military targets, holding the threat of city destruction in reserve, hereby inducing an adversary under pressure of limited attrition and punishment to terminate the war before it escalates to the final holocaust. Such a strategy of controlled response requires central and firm control over the employment of strategic forces and is incompatible with the counter-city strategy that a country with small and relatively vulnerable striking forces is compelled to adopt. As Pierre Messmer, minister of the armed forces of France, admitted recently: "With our means, the only objectives that have a deterrent value are the population objectives. . . . "[4] Finally, if American advice on strengthening NATO's conventional capabilities were accepted, the alliance, and all its members, would be less dependent for its security on the enormously destructive power of nuclear weapons. The inter-allied division of labor implied would offer NATO more choices of response than any one of its members could hope to enjoy if reduced to its national resources. On the military view, no alternative looks nearly so good.

However, one must not rush to the conclusion that the official American position is indisputably sound and that its European critics are unreasonable. If Americans did so conclude, they would be underrating the dilemma that confronts them. If a great many

Europeans feel a lack of dignity in the role of junior partner that their countries are playing, their sentiment is hardly outrageous, especially on the part of Englishmen, Frenchmen, and Germans; and the desire to put oneself out for one's security, to become more self-reliant in matters of defense, is not necessarily an unhealthy posture. More to the point, however, is the doubt that the security and foreign policy interests of all NATO countries are virtually identical. If they are not, the American position rests on a shaky political premise. The past reveals that European and American interests have conflicted on numerous political, economic, and military matters, and some of these differences have concerned issues to which the control of military power is germane. Such divergences of interest are bound to continue and may increase in the future. They could disappear only if the nations involved became politically integrated in an effective political community.

Nor is President de Gaulle unrealistic when he refers to the risk France and Europe run in depending for nuclear protection entirely on an ally. It may seem inconceivable that the United States would ever fail to honor her pledge, once more given eloquently by President Kennedy when he declared in Frankfurt on June 25, 1963: "The United States will risk its cities to defend yours because we need your freedom to protect ours."[5] Yet the circumstances of the United States might change drastically and unpredictably in the future, and if the record of history means anything, it surely supports the General's skepticism and caution. One need not flatly assume, as General Gallois does, that mutual threats of nuclear devastation mean "the end of the systems of collective security."[6] But General Gallois can and does quote several highly placed Americans—such as General Taylor and Mr. Herter[7]—in support of his disbelief in the dependability of United States nuclear protection. A country that has alternatives would be imprudent if it staked its survival squarely on any alliance among sovereign states.

It is in General de Gaulle's insistence on an independent French nuclear force that his policy clashes violently with the American position. To the General such a force is the indispensable basis of military independence and national sovereignty and status. The

45

United States is firmly opposed to the Gaullist design for fear that the proliferation of national nuclear sytems will increase the insecurity of all nations; that the large cost of such forces will prevent smaller countries from making adequate non-nuclear provision for their defense, rendering them overly dependent on what, in terms of real deterrent power, is a suicidal and hence probably incredible threat of reprisal; that what the British and French have cannot long be denied to West Germany; that national nuclear weapons in German hands would present the alliance with a special risk of involvement in nuclear war since she—alone among the NATO countries—is a nation divided by external fiat and not one, therefore, that can be expected to remain a status quo power; and, finally, as already noted, that in the eyes of the United States the best strategy of nuclear deterrence requires highly centralized control and options other than the wholesale destruction of cities.

The technical grounds for this American position against further national nuclear forces seem eminently sound as far as they go. The question is whether this position has any chance of prevailing. Of course, by focusing on Gaullist France, one is looking at the most extreme NATO critic of the United States, and it may be expected that even French policy will become less recalcitrant when General de Gaulle ceases to be President.[8] However, the General may govern for some time to come. Some of his creatures and creations may outlive him as political factors and make any shift in French policy uncertain and slow at best. Moreover, there is a degree of political realism in the French view on the value of alliances. On the other hand, it is hard, though perhaps not impossible, to see how a healthy NATO could function without France, her position being such that she can obstruct and veto when she cannot lead or persuade.

It is often observed by non-Frenchmen that French policy, as it impinges on Europe's security, is unrealistic in terms of resources and is reflective of a vainglorious hankering after a past prestige, after a *grandeur* that—in this modern world—is beyond the reach of France. These observations are persuasive and yet, up to a point, it may be well to suspend judgment.

It is easy enough to point to Britain, which has been possessor of the nuclear bomb for some time and is finding it hard, if not impossible, to assure adequate means of delivery for her nuclear bombs once the aging V-bomber is definitely obsolete. How can the French achieve what the British seem unable to do, and why do the French persist when many informed Englishmen advocate that their own country abandon its strenuous attempts to maintain a national system of nuclear deterrence? No doubt the costs of developing the *force de frappe* are immense, and this may be critical in view of other urgent claims to a larger share in the growing national product voiced by French industrial workers, farmers, and the *salariat.* Even now the French economy is subject to strong inflationary pressures. As France tries to develop the complicated technical components that her bombs and bombers require in order to create a well-functioning and reasonably survivable deterrent system, and to maintain its military worth in the face of a rapidly advancing arms technology, she may well fail to make ends meet and wind up with nuclear armament of negligible military significance. On the other hand, it is not wholly inconceivable that she will outperform England. The comparative potential to construct and operate a national force for strategic reprisal is not measured simply by size of population and gross national product. The French may display more will than Britain has shown to devote resources to defense, and she may use these resources with better direction. Since the war, after all, France has demonstrated a remarkable ability for industrial management and innovation.

Nor should it be taken for granted that the *force de suasion,* if it emerges as an operationally respectable system, would be without military utility for France. True, her capabilities would be dwarfed by those of either Soviet Russia or the United States, and she could hardly hope to exert decisive power of nuclear deterrence vis-à-vis the U.S.S.R. Nevertheless, she could give somewhat more pause to an aggressor than if she were wholly dependent on conventional armament.

There may also be French hopes that a small nuclear force will compel the United States to accept France as a nuclear equal and give her a real share in planning and managing the nuclear capabilities of the entire alliance. Even if such sharing did not come about, some Frenchmen speculate that a small *force de frappe* would permit France in an emergency to trigger the huge forces of the United States. This risk of a French independent capability's forcing the hand of an incomparably stronger ally is, of course, exactly one of the reasons why the United States opposes a number of independent forces in the alliance. If France persists, the United States will no doubt find ways of minimizing the risk that a catalytic agent will usurp her own decision on a matter of supreme import. Nevertheless, some such risk might persist and be regarded as an asset by the French. In any event, there are indications that Gaullist France expects to obtain mainly political rather than strictly military benefits from her nuclear force. As one French general recently put it: "The French strategic nuclear force, isolated and quarantined, as it were, will have a small capability and will be further handicapped by the lack of broad research programs and technological advances, since France can rely only on her own human and budgetary resources. Militarily, its effectiveness will be limited, yet there is every likelihood that it will carry a weight in the diplomatic sphere out of all proportion to its size."[9] It can scarcely be denied that France would be given more heed in any high-level negotiations affecting the security of Europe. This is a point that General de Gaulle has made repeatedly. He made it again during his press conference of July 29, 1963. Almost as if he tried to prove De Gaulle's point, Prime Minister Macmillan told the House of Commons on the same day that the Labour Party's anti-nuclear stand was wrong and that Britain was one of the powers negotiating the test-ban agreement because he and the Conservative government had had the courage to keep Britain a nuclear power. "He said Britain had been at the conference table at Moscow, not by profession of high moral principles, not through anti-bomb demonstrations, not through carrying banners or lying down on the highway to protest against the H-bomb, but rather 'by the right and authority of its own nuclear power.' "[10] In saying this, Macmillan spoke De Gaulle's language. The "right and authority of its own nuclear power" is precisely what the General wants France to have.

But the question must now be asked: even if De Gaulle succeeds against impressive odds in obtaining for himself, and for those

Frenchmen who share his values, the national nuclear foundation for the authority he craves, what will this mean for the security of Europe? As far as one can tell, he envisages the continuation—at least for some time—of the North Atlantic alliance—though an alliance with looser ties than at present, in which France and Britain as well as the United States are independent nuclear powers, and which is less dominated by the United States. He also visualizes France as the leader of a continental federation in which she is the sole owner of national nuclear weapons, and a federation whose interests she represents vis-à-vis what he calls the "Anglo-Saxons."

De Gaulle's conception of a continental confederation of national states accepting the leadership of France—even a nuclear France—is likely to prove unrealistic. The other continental nations are scarcely prepared at present to exchange the protection of the United States for that of France. Whatever the *force de frappe* may do for France, will it look better, say, to the Dutch or Norwegians than the Strategic Air Command? Surely only the most spectacular withdrawal of American backing would induce the Federal Republic of Germany to throw in her lot with France, in the area of defense, rather than the United States, if she had to make a choice. Bonn has made this very clear. The fact is that even with the *force de frappe*, France will not become a power remotely comparable to the U.S.S.R. and the United States. She may be an independent nuclear power but she will be a small nuclear power and this will place severe limits on her independence of action. And, furthermore, there remains the big question mark in regard to France as a political community. What will France be like, how will she function as a political unit when De Gaulle is no longer her sovereign? Surely this grave uncertainty—which baffles Frenchmen as well as non-Frenchmen[11]—must limit the confidence which her neighbors can muster toward France.

If this view is correct, then there can be, on the continent, little French political and military leadership that is pointedly anti-American and anti-British, and though De Gaulle may achieve what is good for France, his ambition may substract from rather than add to the security of western Europe. The General would seriously jeopardize Europe's security if his policy were merely to divide Europe, keep NATO in disarray, and if his imperturbable intransigence caused the United States to reduce its commitment to Europe. Of course, no matter what De Gaulle chooses to do, it would not be rational for the United States to diminish protection of western Europe, and some Frenchmen may well calculate that the selfish American interest in protecting western Europe against Soviet aggression is so strong that it will prevail regardless of what happens to NATO or to Franco-American relations. However, they should not feel too sure. After all, Americans are not immune to reactions of pique, disgust, and anger.

In recent months, the French government may have become aware of its limited room for maneuver as long as France is acting strictly on her own. She has been suffering a degree of isolation in Europe ever since De Gaulle vetoed Britain's entry into the Common Market. One French spokesman threw out the hint in September, 1963, that British co-operation with France in nuclear weaponry might open the door to the Common Market.[12] This hint stirred no visible interest in Britain and it seems extremely improbable, barring spectacular blunders on the part of the United States, that Britain would come to terms with General de Gaulle on a strongly anti-American course of action.

In partial summary, it seems fair to say that General de Gaulle expresses some of the European malaise about the present organization of European security and that this malaise rests on some substantial reasons for dissatisfaction. De Gaulle exploits rather recklessly his negative power in the alliance to veto and disrupt. This may be irksome. But if he insists on a French nuclear capability, he is not immoral and he is acting within his rights as the head of a sovereign state. England, after all, has so far not decided to give up her modest nuclear capability, and the French must chafe under the unequal treatment that the United States has accorded to Britain and France. On the other hand, the General's concept of French leadership in a continental Europe of sovereign nations capable of providing largely for their own security seems utterly unrealistic. There is not one country that has even begun to nibble.

But if the present organization of Western security threatens to become unacceptable to an increasing number of Europeans, what constructive alternatives are there to De Gaulle's course?

Is European political unification such a constructive alternative? De Gaulle's design is, of course, predicated on his belief that a federated Europe is neither practicable nor desirable. Nevertheless, there is the question of whether western Europe could not go far toward assuring its security by means under its own control through effecting its political and military unification—not, of course, in the form of De Gaulle's confederation but in the form of a federation with supranational organs based on supranational consensus. Through such a united structure, the western Europeans could even hope eventually to recover Great Power status and gain a freedom and power of action that might benefit not only Europe but the rest of the world as well. This is the vision of the European movement. And even if—utterly unlike the Gaullists—many Europeans, especially among the younger generation and, of course, on the political Left, are permanently disillusioned with old-fashioned nationalism and the traditional game of power politics played between nation-states; even if they sense that, in order to survive and prosper, mankind must find and experiment with new forms of organization to take on some of the functions traditionally performed by the nation-state; even then they may realize that, in the world as it is now, it takes power, including military power, to make their own preferences secure and to participate effectively in the shaping of a new world order.

Whether such a Europe will ever become a reality is impossible to say. But it could hardly do so, and thereby change the very basis of the European security problem, in any foreseeable future. First of all, this is not General de Gaulle's vision. His motivation is nationalistic and traditional. Denying the feasibility as well as the desirability of a federal structure, he can in fact do a great deal to prove his prophecy correct. His rude veto of Britain's entry into the Common Market has dealt a jolting setback to progressive integration of west European activities, although had Britain joined, she also would have put the brake on any serious attempts at political integration. In any case, De Gaulle's flat rejection of British membership revealed and considerably increased disunity among the Six and especially, despite the solemn conclusion of the Franco-German treaty, disunity between these two big partners. As subsequent negotiations of the Six have demonstrated, there is now a shrinking from closer political alignment and a more determined concentration on national self-interest in coping with the economic and commercial issues of the Community.

More basically, remarkable though the achievement of the Common Market is, it does not imply that political and military unification will follow as a matter of course or that, if they were attempted, success would be likely. The European "communities" thus far established have required sovereign states to exercise their sovereignty in certain agreed-upon ways in certain delimited areas of economic life. If these common structures flourish—and this is not to be taken for granted since they have not stood the test of economic adversity—their inherent momentum may gather force and push integration, step by step, in a variety of fields related to trade. It is also true that the activities of the Common Market do now involve politics and may be said, therefore, to represent a degree of "political community";[13] and, no doubt, a far-reaching economic community embracing monetary management and public investment would presuppose a strong central political authority. It is improbable, however, that this will come into being in the near future, and it is certainly optimistic to say that the European Economic Community "cannot fail to lead to a political Europe by simple functional necessity."[14] In fact, it remains to be seen whether the EEC will ever become much more than a glorified tariff union, reduced perforce to an economic policy of laissez faire. In any case, to merge foreign and military policies is a process penetrating to the very essence of sovereign nationhood. It would be tantamount to merging national sovereignty itself. The merging process would require the effective reconciliation of divergent national interests or, to put it differently, the effective organization of conflicting interests across national boundaries. Though nationalism has declined as a unifying force in western Europe, it has hardly weakened far enough to permit supranational unification now. The observable fact is that the nation-state is at present still the basic political unit in national as well as world politics. Certainly, the desire for European federation is at this time confined to a relatively small minority. The majority of west Europeans can best be described as being quite uncertain about the kind of Europe they want.

This statement is not meant to sound pessimistic or to indicate disbelief in the chance that Europe will eventually unite. However, short of some dramatic and traumatic event that throws the Europeans more closely together, unification could probably occur only on a gradual and pragmatic basis, and in a manner in which no one step compelled the next. It could occur only over a long period of time and it could not therefore form, for many years to come, a foundation for the military independence of western Europe.

If federation does not now look like a feasible solution to the problem of European security, neither—owing to insufficiency of scale—does the independent-national approach, even for Europe's middle powers. A purely west European alliance, leaving out the United States, would be hard to negotiate. Even if it could be negotiated and could elicit from its members a stronger effort than they have been disposed to accept under NATO auspices, an adequate and truly independent capability for deterrence and defense would take a great many years to achieve.

These conditions suggest that Europe's security will continue to require, at least for many years to come, a North Atlantic solution. This assumes, of course, that this familiar alternative looks more attractive to most Europeans—undoubtedly it does—than a neutralist position between the United States and the Soviet Union that would not demand more than small national military capabilities but that would also promise only the most precarious degree of security.

However, a North Atlantic solution, to be viable, must meet some of Europe's demands and criticisms even if it does not satisfy General de Gaulle. The question then becomes one of the evolution of NATO and of the policy pursued by the United States. As long as the United States opposes, for the reasons already mentioned, a plurality of independent systems for nuclear deterrence in NATO, there are two directions in which the United States can move in order to mitigate the American nuclear monopoly and predominance and thus yield to some European pressures. One way would be to lend to NATO allies a share in the management of strategic deterrence; the other would be the establishment of a multilateral nuclear force, independent of the bulk of the American capability, under NATO auspices. Indeed, the United States has made a start along each of these lines.

For example, the United States has recently announced her intention of inviting European officers to the headquarters of SAC at Omaha. It should be possible to give her allies a considerable and increasing participation in the formulation of nuclear strategy and in plans for various contingencies, including strategy for all limited forms of war.[15] But, no matter how far the United States is prepared to travel along this road to co-operation, she dare not follow it to the end at which control over the employment of her strategic forces would be truly multilateral. Aside from other objections, to do so would seriously risk paralyzing the command of those forces and hence undermining their power to deter aggression. Allied control is divided control, and divided control favors inaction, not action. Despite this limiting qualification, a great deal could be achieved along these lines that is not being done now and that would diminish some legitimate European grievances. But it is equally clear that, by itself, this approach is unsatisfactory to General de Gaulle, and might not induce the British to abandon their own forces of deterrence.

This approach could, however, be combined with the establishment of a multilateral nuclear force, provided there is enough European demand for it. Its military utility might look unimpressive to Americans, but Europeans might want it as insurance against the risk, however slight and hypothetical, of receiving insufficient American backing in some future crisis. They might also want it in order to give the United States an extra incentive to share— to some extent—the management of her own strategic capabilities, to assure themselves a more effective voice in matters of arms control and disarmament, and perhaps to enjoy a greater sense of self-reliance. Whatever the degree to which these possible advantages were registered, the management of a multilateral force could also serve as a means to further European political integration and would be welcomed by the proponents of European unification on this account. If one believes in the cause of European unity, though its prospects seem dim at present, one might well ask: Why retrogress with General de Gaulle, who has made it plain that in the realms of defense and foreign policy he wants no supranational nonsense, but a *Europe des patries*? Why not then contemplate a multilateral striking force, if Europe insists on some deterrent capability separate from the American? By building and managing such a force, the European countries would be embarking on another common enterprise, and on one that could have far more built-in supranationality than the Common Market.

To serve these multiple purposes, however, a multilateral force would have to meet two important conditions. First, its constitution would have to offer credible protection in the event of attack not only on the entire membership but also on any individual member. Second, such a force could not tolerate a special American veto, even though it could tolerate, and in fact benefit greatly from, American participation.

Neither condition would be easy to satisfy. Nevertheless, a strong case can be made for giving the idea serious study and making it the subject of imaginative experimentation. Together with America's first approach, it may represent at this time the best available option for Europe and the United States. This is not, of course, certain. The main problem would be the response of France. As of now, it is probable that De Gaulle would refuse even a truly multilateral nuclear system if its acceptance required that the national *force de frappe* be abandoned. Permitting France to build at least a symbolic force of her own, and on her own, might be one price that the rest of the NATO community, and especially the United States, would have to pay in order to make a multilateral force palatable; and they could do so in the hope that some day France would be prepared, along with Britain, to place her force under multilateral control.

The stark fact is that a United States nuclear monopoly, desirable as it is from the American military point of view, cannot be maintained. It is improbable that the British and French will ever abandon their national deterrent forces, except possibly by contributing them to a multilateral system over which the United States has no special veto, and in exchange for some European participation in planning the deterrent posture of the alliance. And in view of differences in national interests, it may well be that Britain and France will hang on to their national forces, at least for some time, no matter what concessions the United States is prepared to make. In that event, it would seem to be in the American interest to put up with this condition and press for as much co-ordination—in terms of a multinational force—as is feasible. On the other hand, the United States might do well to reject the advice of those premature "realists" who regard the development of more national nuclear systems as inevitable and who urge her to fall in with them now, to help them along by assisting national nuclear aspirations, and to begin by helping France entirely on De Gaulle's terms.

No doubt France is at this time the "odd man out" in the NATO framework. De Gaulle's stand—at times harsh and suggestive of a desire to see the alliance break up—is troublesome to all his allies, not just to the United States and, of course, Great Britain. It will be difficult to adjust the alliance in a manner acceptable to him. Yet there is at least one ground on which the General might be met with a degree of sympathy. France might be treated with forbearance because, as everyone knows, she has suffered the rude shocks of ignominious defeat and occupation and—perhaps for this reason—has experienced a decline in international power and the loss of her colonial empire as further blows dealt by a cruel outside world. Caught in the pressures of rapid economic development and social change, she obviously finds it hard to equip herself with a political system that would allow her to function and prosper under the new conditions of this twentieth century. Indeed, it has been suggested that *grandeur* in international affairs is to De Gaulle not so much an end as a means of making the French people pull together as a nation.[16]

There are also two reasons for dealing with the French challenge constructively. It would be healthier for the entire West if the

European nations in NATO would express more initiative in the area of defense and provide more resources, moral as well as material, for security, and hence pull more military weight in the alliance. The second reason is closely related. Now that western Europe as a whole has recovered wealth, vigor, and poise, it should not be expected in the future to buckle under to the United States as it did in the past. Europe requires and will demand more room for initiative in coping with the outside world on the military and political, as well as on the economic and cultural, levels. Only if western Europe gains some greater measure of control over her security and destiny will she, or at any rate some of her members, cease to act as military-client states, leaving much of the inconvenient defense business to the big ally across the ocean.

The fact is that France regards NATO in its present form as an organization designed to perpetuate United States domination over the national security of the West. This might be acceptable if what is called the Atlantic Community could become, and could soon become, a political as well as military reality. After all, these are realities that, to endure, must be complementary. But although the United States is inclined to regard traditional national sovereignty as obsolete in Europe, it is extremely jealous of her own and hardly prepared to push Atlantic political integration to a point comparable with the military integration on which she insists.

This view, if it is right, makes it incumbent on the United States to find other ways of transforming NATO into a more responsible partnership—though not, of course, one of equal partners—and this calls, above all, for new arrangements in the matter of nuclear power. The directions in which the United States might probe and press are fairly clear. No matter through which combination of military power and arms control security will be served best, both western Europe and the United States can be more secure within some sort of North Atlantic framework than by going it alone.

1. Reprinted in the *Atlantic Community Quarterly*, I (1963), 178.
2. *New York Times*, July 30, 1963, p. 10.
3. *Ibid.*

4. Pierre Messmer, "France's Military Policy," *Military Review*, XLIII (August, 1963), 26.

5. *Christian Science Monitor*, June 26, 1963, p. 4.

6. Pierre M. Gallois, "The Trap Offered De Gaulle," *Bulletin of the Atomic Scientists*, XIX (October, 1963), 24.

7. Pierre M. Gallois, "The *Raison d'Être* of French Defense Policy," *International Affairs*, XXXIX (October, 1963), 502 f.

8. According to a public-opinion poll that asked respondents to state whether they favored French participation in the test-ban treaty "even if it would interrupt France's nuclear armaments program," only 10 per cent were against signing the treaty, while 53 per cent were in favor of doing so. *New York Herald Tribune* (European edition), September 19, 1963, p. 1.

9. General Paul Stehlin, "The Evolution of Western Defense," *Foreign Affairs*, XLII (October, 1963), 78.

10. *Christian Science Monitor*, July 30, 1963, p. 1.

11. See the perceptive chapters by Stanley Hoffmann, Jean-Baptiste Duroselle, and François Goguel in Stanley Hoffmann *et al.*, *In Search of France* (Cambridge, Mass., 1963).

12. Speech by M. Habib-Deloncle at Strasbourg, September 23, 1963.

13. Cf. Walter Hallstein, "The European Economic Community," *Political Science Quarterly*, LXXVIII (June, 1963), 165; Ernst Friedlaender and Katharina Focke, *Europa über den Nationen* (Cologne, 1963), p. 76.

14. Jean-Charles Snoy, "The European Crisis," *Atlantic Community Quarterly*, I (1963), 139.

15. For a forceful advocacy of such a course, see Alastair Buchan, "The Reform of NATO," *Foreign Affairs*, XLI (January, 1962), 179 ff.

16. Stanley Hoffmann, "De Gaulle's Memoirs: The Hero of History," *World Politics*, XIII (October, 1960), 150–51.

French Politicians and the European Communities: The Record of the 1950's   HANS A. SCHMITT

THE TUMULTUOUS HISTORY of modern Europe has witnessed constant stirrings of the visionary spirit which attempted to end strife and division and tried to replace national multiplicity with continental cohesion. Frenchmen played a prominent part in this movement, ever since the Abbé Saint-Pierre elicited both praise and ridicule at the Peace of Utrecht for his project of European pacification.[1] Advocates of peace and order carried his vision like a banner through the eighteenth century, and even a pessimist like Voltaire came to believe that the worthy cleric's spirit had contributed to the birth of a European Republic of Letters. Ideologers of the French Revolution were not content merely to emancipate their nation but hoped to build on this beginning a universal republic of free men.[2] Not even the chilling winds of the Restoration discouraged the Comte de Saint-Simon's faith in the ultimate construction of a European commonwealth resting on popular consent and governed by continental Lords and Commons. Napoleon III was ever conscious of an inheritance that featured not only the memory of Marengo and Austerlitz but the vision of an empire of peace and harmony as well. It was during the dying days of the Second Empire that the League for Peace and Freedom was founded, at whose first meeting in 1869 Victor Hugo eulogized the United States of Europe. A Frenchman, Charles Lemonnier, nurtured this flickering flame of idealism through the half-century from the Peace of Frankfurt to the Treaty of Versailles.

The only serious attempt between two world wars to replace the comity of sovereign national states with a European federation originated in France. Edouard Herriot and Aristide Briand were its most prominent advocates. On September 5, 1929, the latter—then foreign minister—presented his plan for a confederation of European states to the League of Nations. He hoped to implement this project through the aegis of two agencies: a legislative conference and an executive committee. Throughout the 1920's French scholars and thinkers had prepared the way for his great public pronouncement. In 1920, Albert Demangeon, professor of geography at the Sorbonne, warned that Europe could only maintain her place in the world if she pooled her economic, political, and human resources. Business leaders like Louis Loucheur and Lacour-Gayet advocated multilateral reduction of tariffs as a beginning in the fight against economic nationalism. Both the Herriot and Painlevé governments associated themselves with the Pan-European idea, and the periodical *L'Europe de Demain*, founded in 1927, counted in its executive committee Briand, Herriot, Loucheur, Yves la Troquer and Francis Delaisi. During every significant economic conference between 1927 and 1931, representatives of this group unveiled plans for a European economic union, and in 1930 they organized in Paris the First Congress for a European Tariff Union. On the intellectual plane Drieu de la Rochelle's *Mesure de la France* echoed the fear that Europe would be swallowed by the emergent world powers of East and West unless the peoples of the continent found strength and vision to unite.[3]

Everyone realizes today that Briand's *beau geste* had been preceded by too much talking and had come ten years too late. The first postwar decade of opportunity was about to founder in world depression and submerge in a new wave of lawlessness. Briand's great speech to the League was the last act of a long and not always glorious career. The certainty of its uselessness was all the French statesman took to his grave in 1932.[4]

Fittingly enough, the newspaper *Combat*, organ of the French Resistance, first revived the idea of the United States of Europe in 1942.[5] Once more the seed of European freedom was planted on

French soil. Thanks to this pronouncement the courageous leaders of the oppressed in many occupied countries came to embrace more than the elementary desire to liberate their peoples. The Resistance committed itself to the principle of reform as well as restoration.

The postwar years brought no rapid implementation of the idea, but the aim was not abandoned, especially not in France. "From 1946 to 1954, the initiatives [toward European Union] came almost always from France, particularly those which were to constitute the most decisive advances towards a Europe equipped with functioning institutions, both in the economic and the political sector."[6] First in this succession of achievement stood the Hague Congress convoked in 1948 by the International Committee of Movements for European Unity. Here, at last, emerged the summary demand for a supranational government superimposed on a European federation. This wish was supported by the large French delegation led by Georges Bidault, Léon Blum, Paul Ramadier, Paul Reynaud, and Robert Schuman. Denis de Rougemont was the author of the final document which summarized the aspirations of the Congress.[7]

The Hague Congress gave birth to the Council of Europe, not yet the community dreamed of, but a forum where its realization could be furthered. Everyone knows that its headquarters were established on French soil, in Strasbourg. The first meeting of its Consultative Assembly saw Edouard Herriot in the chair. From 1952-54 its labors were guided by François de Menthon (Mouvement Républicain Populaire), who was succeeded by Guy Mollet, the French Socialist leader. France sent anything but backbenchers to Strasbourg. René Coty was one of the original delegation of eighteen, joined by men like Bidault, Edouard Bonnefous, Mollet, Reynaud, Maurice Schuman, and Pierre-Henri Teitgen.[8] The first two secretaries-general of the Consultative Assembly, Jacques-Camille Paris and Léon Marchal, were likewise recruited in France. Nor would this record be complete if one omitted the numerous projects deposited and the numerous debates led by Frenchmen, all aiming at the initiation or implementation of some concrete step toward European union. A cynical review of the calendar might almost tempt one to suspect that authorship of some "European Plan" had become the indispensable status symbol of political leadership among prominent Socialists, Catholics, and Moderates in the National Assembly.

In the very first session of the Consultative Assembly, the Socialist André Philip and the Independent Paul Reynaud demanded the "creation of a political authority of supranational character."[9] Edouard Bonnefous (UDSR), at the time chairman of the National Assembly's Committee on Foreign Relations, advocated a European Transport Organization, a project revived two years later by Maurice Lemaire, the Gaullist senator from the Vosges. Pierre Pflimlin (MRP), the perennial minister of agriculture of the Fourth Republic, became the equally indefatigable advocate of the "pool vert," a common market for agriculture, while Paul Ribeyre, minister of public health in the Pleven (1951) and Pinay (1952) cabinets, sponsored a plan for a European Health Authority.[10]

In the end these drafts, proposals, and suggestions were overshadowed by the plan of yet another Frenchman, Robert Schuman. On May 3, 1950, the late French foreign minister received from Jean Monnet, France's planning commissioner, the draft of a proposal designed to stall Europe's return to fruitless rivalry and cyclical depression. The seasoned Alsatian veteran, whose native soil had been the scene of many wars, responded to the idea of pooling the heavy industrial resources of Germany and France and, six days later, announced to the world that the labor of Monnet's planners had been elevated to the status of French national policy. Another French initiative on Europe's behalf was begun.

Within a year the Schuman Plan ripened into a treaty signed by six nations (France, Germany, Italy, Belgium, Holland, and Luxembourg), and in the fall of 1952 a supranational governing body, the High Authority, a parliamentary assembly, and a court of justice began to operate what is now known as the European Coal and Steel Community. Conceived by Frenchmen, supported by France, often with unbending severity, it now entered the phase of reality when the leadership and wisdom of six nations would have to assume responsibility for its functioning.

According to the treaty establishing the European Coal and Steel Community, no nation was to pre-empt more than two seats on the nine-man executive board. Eight of these men were initially appointed by the governments, the ninth to be chosen by these men by co-option. France and Germany each furnished two members. The election through the co-optive process of the Belgian labor leader Paul Finet resulted in a similar privileged position for that country, leaving the High Authority with two members each from the most important producer nations.[11]

Until the establishment of the European Economic Community and Euratom, a French member presided over the labors of the High Authority: first, Jean Monnet, a case of the father's teaching his infant how to walk; and then, after his resignation in 1955, ex-Premier René Mayer. The list of additional French members has included Léon Daum (1952–59), past director-general of the Homecourt steel complex (Compagnie des Forges et Acieries de la Marine) and a member of the boards of various other heavy industrial enterprises in France and the Saar; Roger Reynaud, who replaced Mayer in 1958, though not as president, and who was a leader in the French Christian labor movement; and following Daum's resignation in 1959, the Socialist Pierre-Oliver Lapie, former minister of education and vice-president of the National Assembly.

This French executive contingent included politicians and men whose precise ideological positions were unknown. Neither Monnet nor Daum had any party affiliation. Although one might assume that Reynaud would vote for the MRP candidate in his district, he has not been explicitly associated with that party. Only Mayer and Lapie have been party men who could look back on long stints in parliament and as cabinet ministers. The indeterminate political coloration of the group indicates that these appointments were intended to represent something more than political opinions. The Monnet-Daum duo exhibited several positive attributes: Monnet was the true founding father and the head of the delegation that had negotiated the treaty establishing the community.[12] Daum, on the other hand, was deliberately chosen to represent conservative business interests, and to encourage their support of the new venture. After the French rejection of the European Defense Community had convinced Monnet that the European concept was again in danger and required his help on other fronts, he tendered his resignation. The next appointment was, therefore, crucial in two respects. After the governments had agreed that the next French incumbent would also succeed to the presidency, the new appointee would have to be comparable to the planner from Cognac in prominence, as well as in dedication, to the new order. Mayer was acceptable on both counts. His commitment to European integration was beyond question. His association with the Parisian circles of high finance and his important role in the profitable nationalization of the railroads of northern France served to increase business support to the community. His immediate political past placed him in the forefront of the leaders of the Fourth Republic. Clearly, France intended to continue sending her first team to Luxembourg. But the High Authority's prestige crisis had not been solved. When Mayer resigned in 1958 and Daum departed the following year, it loomed larger than ever.

It has been generally assumed that Mayer's retirement and return to private business signified the end of an era. Following the inauguration of the Rome treaties, it was not only clear that ECSC had weathered the EDC crisis, but that Europe was moving another step forward. Mayer's job was done. From 1955 to 1958 he had held a unique position as president of the only European community *in extremis*. Since ECSC could expect to be overshadowed by the more ambitious Common Market of the European Economic Community, a man of his past and prominence was bound to consider retirement—he was sixty-three—or other fields of activity. His successor, accordingly, was a far younger and far less eminent labor leader who had also been a high civil-service official in the ministry of finance, though not at the directoral level. With his accession, the presidency of the High Authority passed from French to Belgian hands, Paul Finet's. In 1959, Daum's resignation did not result in a comparable comedown (Lapie was probably much better known) but in an inexplicable shift to the left.[13] As in the case of Reynaud, however, the new French member became a simple private in the ranks, holding neither the presidency nor either of the two vice-presidencies.

Thus, the French role in the High Authority has become more modest, and the political coloration of the membership has changed from the days of Daum and Mayer, two men with big-business connections, and is now comprised of two men of the moderate Left. While the political shift is unique, the parallel decline in prominence has had a counterpart in the more modest role that has been played by the German members since the resignation of the German vice-president Franz Etzel in 1957. During the last five years the presidency of the High Authority has passed from a Belgian to an Italian, while the two vice-presidencies have been held by a Belgian (Albert Coppé) and a Netherlander (Dirk Spierenburg), respectively. Germany and France have had other fish to fry and have inherited the presidencies of EEC and Euratom, while the comparative backwater of ECSC has provided opportunities to redress the patronage balance, on paper at least, in favor of the smaller nations.

Among French personalities on the High Authority, Monnet and Mayer had no equals. Outwardly, the former came close to a position of charismatic leadership among dedicated Europeans. Whether it is true, as rumored, that he had expected to find in the High Authority a body composed of himself and eight rubber stamps, it is extremely difficult to determine. In any case, men like Franz Etzel of Germany, Dirk Spierenburg of the Netherlands, and Paul Finet of Belgium, were soon equally active and almost equally prominent in the European arena. If Monnet's resignation was due in part to the frustrations of an incurable autocrat, the succession of Mayer could be said to have improved the team spirit of the High Authority. Here was, certainly, a man more versed in the arts of political leadership, an articulate spokesman and quick-witted debater, endowed with social charm and agility largely lacking in Monnet. If Monnet exemplified the spirit of a leader, Mayer cut the figure of one to an eminent degree. Beside these two men, Daum remained a patient, kindly work horse for industrial relations. Reynaud and Lapie so far seem to have filled two places without contributing notably to the stature of the High Authority in the European constellation.

Since 1958, the center of the stage has been dominated by the Commission of EEC and, though to a lesser extent, Euratom. It is well known that both of these bodies are much less independent of national governments than the High Authority. Therefore, technical competence could be expected to be a more crucial qualification for their membership than the capacity for independent statesmanship. The complexion of the French membership would tend to bear this out.

The first two French members of EEC were somewhat paler images of the initial appointees to the ECSC High Authority. First there was Robert Marjolin, one of the vice-presidents of the Community, an outstanding product of the stable of brilliant young men collected by Jean Monnet in the French Commissariat du Plan. He had been assistant commissioner-general in that office and departed in 1948 to become at the age of thirty-seven secretary-general of the Organization of European Economic Co-operation (OEEC). From Brussels Marjolin has been a prominent and incisive spokesman on questions of international economics and has maneuvered boldly in the explosive sector of EEC expansion, as well as in the settlement of the current chicken-war.[14] At his side, France placed a man almost twenty years his senior, Robert Lemaignen, whose life has been spent in industry and in service on a variety of managing boards of French-African enterprises, and who had also been vice-president of the International Chamber of Commerce. He relinquished these posts to assume a seat on the EEC commission and then, much to the distress of dedicated Europeans, resigned in 1962 to return to the pursuit of his private interests. His place was taken by Henri Rochereau, Independent senator from the Vendée since 1946, member of the European Parliament, and for many years chairman of the Economic Committee of the Council of the Fourth Republic. In 1959, Rochereau became minister of agriculture but was replaced in 1961 during a reshuffling whose chief purpose was "to get more vigorous leadership" into the ministry over which he had presided.[15] This new appointment removed from the EEC scene a representative of private enterprise who had also been an expert on Eurafrican relations. The shift made sense when one considered that a viable basis for continuing contacts between the Community and the emergent African nations had been found, and that there was increasing preoccupation in Brussels and in the national capitals with the problems of agricultural integration. From the outside, it would seem that the shifting kaleidoscope of Common Market problems called for the replacement of an overseas expert by a seasoned veteran in agricultural politics. Whether the selection of a man who had been notably unable to solve agricultural probems on the national level was a proper one might well be doubted.

After ceding the presidency of the High Authority of ECSC to the smaller nations, international arithmetic invested Germany with the presidency of the Commission of EEC, while the leadership of Euratom was to devolve upon a Frenchman. The executive commission of that body consisted of only five members: each community country except Luxembourg contributed one representative. Despite the French chairmanship of this pioneer venture, three different individuals have held this post during the past five years. First appointed was Louis Armand, president of the French National Railroads, who in 1957 had co-authored a report on the future of atomic energy in western Europe, compiled at the request of the six members of ECSC. An insider in Brussels has described Armand as "volatile, energetic . . . the brilliant scientist engineer who had modernized the state railways, reported on Atomic energy prospects . . . and incidentally invented the name 'Euratom.' "[16] But within a year of assuming his post he was reported to be "sick and overtired" and he resigned on February 2, 1959. Despite rumors that Armand was afflicted with cancer, he shortly acceded to the presidency of one of the largest mining enterprises in Lorraine, a position which the French Who's Who for 1962–63 still reports him as occupying.

Armand's replacement was another distinguished member of the Monnet team. Etienne Hirsch had entered the office of the Commissariat du Plan in 1946 and succeeded Monnet as commissioner-general in 1952.[17] While Armand had been in office only briefly, and even then showed no significant intent to function as a vigorous policy-maker or spokesman, Hirsch revealed himself as a person of enthusiasm and vigor. However, his earnest dedication to the European ideal ran counter, so it seems, to the policies of the French government, and at the expiration of his term in January, 1962, he was not reappointed, though he had let it be known that he would gladly continue to serve. In a much-quoted farewell address before the European Parliament he reassured his many friends who mourned his departure that he would "continue with all forces at my command to promote the creation of the United States of Europe . . . essential for the progress of our peoples and the preservation of world peace."[18]

Hirsch's successor, Pierre Chatenet, is a rare French civil servant, who in 1959 was elevated to the Ministry of the Interior. It is generally presumed that he can be expected to follow policies considered safe by the present French regime. This last French appointment involves a person who has never been caught looking beyond the confines of France. He has not had the international business experience of a Lemaignen or the international administrative career of a Marjolin or a share in the labors of the European Parliament like Rochereau. Whether his appointment will be followed by others of the same kind remain to be seen. If so, one might be tempted to conclude that "l'Europe des nations" is not only a concept designed to slow down the political unification of Europe, but also to dilute and possibly reverse the economic integration of the western half of the continent.

The French members of the EEC and Euratom commissions include neither a Monnet nor a person boasting the political experience of a René Mayer. The man who has contributed most to the progress and dynamism of the institutions themselves has been Robert Marjolin, a good European and an economist of world reputation. His speeches before the European Parliament have put into vivid relief a razor-sharp mind whose possessor can communicate well with laymen. Within the community he appears to have been highly effective, both as an individual and as a spokesman for the Commission.[19] Like Marjolin, as has been indicated, Hirsch did much to capture the European imagination. His dismissal has been a blow comparable almost to the French defeat of EDC. Lemaignen and Rochereau do not emerge from the shadow of the official texts. They have provided certain types of needed expertise, and that would seem to be the only conclusion warranted at this time. Chatenet must be given time before judgments are passed. Whatever his personal merits and accomplishments, the verdicts no doubt will be affected by the certainty that he symbolizes a French policy which seems a reversion to the old-fashioned view that the new European Commissions are a sum-total of six national interests or—more succinctly—a return from supranational to international organization. At this rate, the French members on the executive bodies of EEC and Euratom may soon be overshadowed by their German colleagues, such as Walter Hallstein and Heinz Krekeler, and by several good Europeans from the Low Countries: Jean Rey of Belgium, Sicco Mansholt and Emmanuel Sassen of the Netherlands. The decline of the High Authority may repeat itself.

This summary of events in the executive sector of the European communities warrants one concluding observation: eleven Frenchmen have served on the executive bodies of the European Commissions. Only four of these had any discernible political affiliation: Lapie, Socialist; Mayer, Radical; Reynaud, probably MRP; and Rochereau, Independent. Each executive has directly or indirectly felt the influence of Jean Monnet, and it is still felt by the EEC commission. While the case of Euratom would indicate that the French government frowns on Frenchmen going overboard for Europe, the continued presence of Marjolin at EEC, and of Lapie at ECSC, would indicate that prejudices on that score have not yet hardened into a rigid policy. One might also add that the Fifth Republic has not been notably more interested than the Fourth in providing direct business representation on the commissions. What one can say with some degree of assurance is that the quality of French representation has declined. Reynaud and Lapie have not been so effective as Monnet, Mayer or Daum. Chatenet's background does not hold the promise of Armand nor the prospect of performance obtained from Etienne Hirsch. Lemaignen and Rochereau were not up to the initial appointments to the High Authority. Robert Marjolin remains as the lone representative of dynamic French leadership in the integration of Europe.

II

At this point the student of the European communities encounters a problem derived from a peculiar and incurable maldistribution of sources. The activity of the executive bodies can be followed on the basis of press releases and annual reports. Their meetings are not public, however, and minutes, if kept, are not open to inspection. Interviews and educated guesses are the only supplements of the official and press record. As this inquiry turns next to the Common Assembly and its successors, the European Parliament, the researcher is overwhelmed by a host of source materials: the stenographic report of the debates, committee reports, relevant debates in national parliaments, and if he is fortunate, he may even be favored with a look into the committee minutes. As a result the scholar may devote to the activities of the Assembly an amount of space quite out of proportion to its importance, or if he wishes to avoid this error, he is faced by the forbidding task of summarizing a great deal into very little. The latter will be attempted here.[20]

In the Common Assembly, the parliamentary organ of ECSC, France, Germany, and Italy occupied eighteen seats each; the Netherlands and Belgium ten each; and Luxembourg four. The French delegation was by far the most divided, representing nine distinct political parties compared with Germany's three, Italy's five, Belgium's three, the Netherlands' four, and Luxembourg's three. Thanks to a more streamlined party organization within the Assembly itself, it was forced into greater cohesion. The Common Assembly recognized only groups with a minimum of nine members, a condition met by the Christian Democrats, Socialists, and Liberals. The first of these accommodated the three French members of the MRP, including the former minister of justice and prosecutor at the Nuremberg War Crimes trial, De Menthon. The second was supported by four French socialists in the Assembly, while the Liberal group became the catch basin for ten more Gallic representatives. In the latter group one encountered such unlikely bedfellows as four Independents, René Pleven of the UDSR, two other representatives of similar splinter groups, and two Radical Socialists who would not be caught dead in the company of either Catholics, Protestants, or Socialists. This leaves out of account the eighteenth French member, Michel Debré, who in those days would not be caught dead with anybody, and who refused to join any political group.[21]

Obviously, the French have dominated among the Liberals to whose slender minority of fourteen, out of a total of seventy-eight, they contributed the lion's share. Until his death in 1957 the group was led by Yvon Delbos. Since that time the mantle has fallen on René Pleven who has weathered the mighty influx of the UNR (Union pour la Nouvelle République) which in the days of the European Parliament has caused the Liberal group to more than double in size.[22] The French Independent, André Mutter, has perennially functioned as secretary. The Christian Democrats, accounting for roughly half of the Assembly's membership, diplomatically bestowed the chairmanship on a member from the BeNeLux area. Throughout the history of the Common Assembly, they were guided first by a Dutch and then by a Belgian member. The Socialists, whose group has fluctuated in the low twenties, have had the misfortune of seeing one leader after another lured away by the blandishments of higher office. More important, the four Frenchmen among this group have played an outstanding role. Guy Mollet first presided until his elevation to the presidency of the French Council of Ministers called him back to Paris. When his successor Henri Fayat became Belgian minister of foreign trade the following year, another Frenchman, Pierre-Olivier Lapie, took over. In the wake of his electoral defeat the group at last became stabilized under a German chairman, Willy Birkelbach, who retired from parliamentary life in 1964.

If the French have done exceedingly well in applying their weight as factional leaders, they were less successful when it came to gathering in key committee assignments. Although constituting 23.1 per cent of the membership of the Common Assembly, they obtained

71

only 16 per cent of the committee chairmanships, compared with 24 per cent for Germany and a disproportinate 28 per cent for Belgium, which only furnished 12.8 per cent of the total of seventy-eight Assembly members. Their pursuit of reportorial assignments has provided them with a fairer share. Frenchmen delivered 23.5 per cent of the committee reports delivered before the parliamentary gathering of ECSC.[23]

But statistics alone do not tell the story. On which committees were Frenchmen key figures, either functionally or personally? Guy Mollet played a determinant role in establishing the committee structure. André Mutter acted as *rapporteur* for the provisional constitutional committee. On the floor, Paul Reynaud was a particularly prominent and articulate spokesman for the European aspirations exemplified by the Assembly.[24] Christian Democrat Alain Poher chaired the Committee for Questions of the Common Market. Pierre-Henri Teitgen and René Pleven were frequent spokesmen for the Foreign Relations Committee of the Common Assembly. Senator André Armengaud carried much weight on the Investment and Finance Committee, while he presided over the Assembly Committee for Budget and Administration. The Socialist Gilles Gozard headed not only the Committee on Commercial Policy, but in 1958 he also delivered its report on the Community's cartel woes, an effort which may have been quoted more often than any one report delivered during the short history of the Common Assembly.

A visitor to the meetings of the Common Assembly before its absorption into the European Parliament might well have come away with the impression that the meeting was ordinarily dominated by the French, but that their Belgian and Dutch friends had to run interference for them frequently when the disorders of their own government called them back from the European to the national plane. However, even so brief and cursory a survey encountered additional and more tangible evidence of this French predominance. Several French liberals became at the European level successful spokesmen for national interests. They used the podium to plead for the canalization of the Moselle, which, it was hoped, would facilitate movement of French ore to German markets, and they have seen their dream come true. This same group urged, again with success, wider European participation in African investments. André Mutter did not hesitate to demand that the French presence continue in the Saar mines even after that territory was returned to Germany.[25] The right to address questions to the High Authority was used more extensively by Frenchmen than by any other national group. Here the Gaullist dissidents, Michel Debré, Jacques Vendroux, and André Krieger, accounted for three-fourths of the queries.[26] Negators of the European spirit though they were, theirs was another way of buttressing the impression of French ascendancy. Germans and Italians by contrast gave the impression of being eager and willing disciples who would have to give themselves some time before they might catch up on the parliamentary expertise of their more fortunate northern and western colleagues. In the case of Germany, one must add that this did not keep the Christian Democrat Hans Furler from functioning as a capable if unspectacular Assembly president. In the case of the Italians, the negative impression was rather deepened by the national parliament's inability to decide who should represent it in Strasbourg, as a result of which Italian absenteeism in the Common Assembly was notorious.

A balance of power was bound to establish itself with the passing of time. Its coming was aided by the conversions of the parliamentary structure following the enactment of the Rome Treaties and by the changes which the coup d'etat of 1958 wrought in France.

When it became known that the treaties establishing EEC and Euratom would each provide for a parliamentary assembly in their framework of institutions, a great deal of pressure was successfully brought on the governments to expand the Common Assembly so that it would serve all three communities. The spectacle of five different assemblies, largely identical in membership and representing in part the same nations, would have been both ludicrous and confusing.[27] The sensible and effective protest resulted in the European Parliament to which France, Germany, and Italy sent contingents of thirty-six members each, while Belgium and the Netherlands claimed fourteen seats each, and Luxembourg six. New talent and a new generation from the former Axis countries, as well as the expansion in numbers, were bound to change the complexion of the enlarged European Diet.

The political coloration of the French delegation changed greatly as a result of the events of 1958. The most recent yearbook of the European Parliament reveals that the number of MRP members (three) and Socialists (four) has remained constant although the size of the national aggregation has doubled. This means that Frenchmen constitute less than 5 per cent of the Christian Democrat group of sixty-four, while they account for roughly 12 per cent of the Socialist faction, now the smallest of the three with thirty-three members. On the other hand, the twenty-eight French senators and deputies that have affiliated with the Liberals occupy more than 60 per cent of a total of forty-three seats. Twenty-two of these are either members of UNR (twelve) or Independents (ten), a distribution which illustrates that the moderate French Right plays a decisive role on the Liberal side of the European Parliament. For the first time a faction of this body can be controlled by members from one country.[28]

As a result it comes as no surprise that the president of the Liberal group is French, although this incumbent, René Pleven, is not a Gaullist but one of the very few French holdovers from the pioneering days of the Common Assembly. A second French deputy, Guy Jarrosson (Independent), holds a seat on the Liberal's executive committee of seven. The Christian Democrats, although almost completely bereft of Frenchmen, are still led by a member of the MRP, Alain Poher. It is again noteworthy that this French senator is another of the select group that can claim charter membership in the Common Assembly of 1952.[29]

In the realm of committee activities the French role has continued to be relatively modest. In the first year of the European Parliament the French held three committee chairmanships out of a total of fourteen; the Germans five; and the Belgians three. Because of the upheavals of 1958, only one committee report out of thirty-two was delivered by a French member.

The picture for the 1960-61 session revealed greater balance. At this point the distribution of committee chairmanships gave Germany four; France and Italy three each; and Belgium, the Netherlands, and Luxembourg one each. This tabulation points to a growing tendency to consider a country's size and power in the assignment of these posts. If further investigation should bear this out, one would be forced to conclude that the Common Assembly had exemplified a more vigorous European spirit than its successor. The distribution of committee reports followed a less consistent pattern. The French gained ground, delivering twelve out of seventy-one reports for the session; but they were still running behind Germany with nineteen, and Belgium with eighteen, while another dozen emanated from Dutch authorship.[30]

These figures raise a host of questions—and answer very few. Has the calibre of French representation in the European Parliament declined as it has in the executive bodies? Evidence so far collected leads to an affirmative reply. The best-known members of the present contingent are men like Robert Schuman,[31] René Pleven, and Alain Poher. Among the newcomers only Maurice Faure, actually a veteran of considerable service in the Assembly,[32] and General Edward Corniglion-Molinier (UNR) are well known beyond the confines of their country, but the latter ceased to be a member in December, 1961. The presence of Jacques Vendroux (UNR), brother-in-law of General de Gaulle, might be an indication, on the other hand, that the new regime will at least occasionally dispatch a personage of weight. French government policy on this matter cannot be determined on the basis of community sources. One reason for the absence of many veterans of the first European battles is simply that they have lost their seats in the French parliament. Teitgen and Lapie, for instance, fell victim to electoral displeasure. The appearance on the French political scene of this new and unprecedentedly powerful party, the Union pour la Nouvelle République (UNR), made a substantial turnover in the delegation and the appearance of many new faces inevitable.

The new French *équipe* did not dominate the European Parliament as the old Europeans had lorded over the Common Assembly. Rousing speeches for the cause were rare, as rare as were the pro-Europeans that made them. As long as Teitgen and Lapie were in their seats, they could be depended on to advocate that union to which they eventually sacrificed their domestic political fortunes. Senator Poher has carried on since their disappearance, assisted with vigor by Maurice Faure and occasionally with diffidence by René Pleven. Gaullist dissent has obviously become more frequent, but its case is no longer stated with the vigor and color mustered by Michel Debré. Even as opponents of the European dream, the French have lost in stature what they have gained in numbers; but the stature is there, staid and predominently conservative when Jacques Vendroux rises to address the membership, or shrill and not always to the point when presented by young Christian Lunet de la Malène, a UNR deputy from Seine since 1958.

Another evidence, if not of a decline at least of a limitation of French influence, may be found in the curious fact that French participation in debate has largely been confined to two issues: agriculture and the relationship with the overseas territories. The chairmanship of the committee on agriculture has habitually been assigned to a Frenchman who has made himself the spokesman for the family farm. In this endeavor the men from Gaul have often risen to spectacular heights of eloquence. During a debate on the problems of radioactivity, Deputy André Boutemy even pleaded for the safety of plants and animals, explaining with the logical finesse characteristic of his nation that the term "population" included them also.[33] On several occasions the same speaker predicated the ultimate success of the European dream on the Commissions' and Assembly's assigning an honored and honorable place to the farmer. Above all, he has insisted that the Community must prevent the farmer from being degraded to the status of an employee in agricultural industry.[34] To warnings from other members, including the atypical MRP deputy René Charpentier, that the Community must not saddle itself with the disastrous burdens of supporting a non-viable agriculture as the United States has done, the Independent and former minister of agriculture Roland Boscary-Monservin airily replied: "If our agricultural policy is going to be determined by material considerations, we are certain to fail."[35] Again and again French members have taken the floor to claim that "taking care of the farmer" was possibly the most important task of EEC.[36]

The French delegation seemed to be equally interested in having EEC rebuild the bridges between Europe and Africa which their own recent failures had helped to burn. At the very first meeting of the European Parliament René Pleven and Hamani Diori (Algeria) successfully sponsored a resolution which demanded that the EEC's Economic and Social Committee institute a special section for the overseas territories.[37] Alain Peyrefitte repeatedly identified Africa as the battlefield where the Community must meet and defeat expanding Chinese influence.[38] General Corniglion-Molinier added that the Soviets were not wont to debate their attitude toward Africa: they had simply gone ahead in 1959 and bought the banana crop of Guinea for the next three years at a fixed price.[39] To several Frenchmen, the continuing association with Africa meant nothing less than securing Europe's southern flank against the common enemy, a doctrine once again formulated and propounded with warmth and eloquence by several of their representatives.[40]

Sound and worthwhile as all these arguments may have been, the fact that the overwhelming majority of French interventions were confined to these two issues in which national interest enjoyed a predominant priority testifies to a changing French position in the European spectrum. In a word, Frenchmen spoke less in the European Parliament than they had in the Common Assembly, and when they intervened they preferred to talk about themselves.

One must add that any comparison of the role and quality of the French membership in the European Parliament must take into account that the power of the French National Assembly has been reduced under the Fifth Republic. Parliamentary seats offer less opportunity to ambitious men, and the result is bound to affect French participation in the labors at Strasbourg. As a result there exists the paradox of continued French leadership in the political groups, involving men who are really no longer powerful in the country which sent them, while the floor is increasingly monopolized by deputies from the other members of the Community.

France's uncertain future role within the European communities was until very recently symbolized by Robert Schuman. When the European Parliament convened for its first meeting, the governments let it be known that they would prefer the election of an Italian to the presidency, since in 1958 the three executives were headed by a Belgian, a Frenchman, and a German, while the presidency of the Court reposed in the hands of Judge A. M. Donner of the Netherlands. The deputies, imbued with the conviction that the Parliament must above all be independent, rose in revolt and elected Schuman instead. His term ended in 1960 and culminated in a touching ceremony in which the European Parliament not only paid tribute to the contributions of this elder statesman to its own deliberations but also honored him in a rousing round of speeches commemorating the tenth anniversary of May 9, 1950, when he had accepted the paternity of European union. Many fine compliments were addressed to him, several of them by French comrades-in-arms who were understandably disturbed about the future. Maurice Faure, rather than one of the many UNR representatives, spoke for the Liberals. Alain Poher recalled that he had stood at the battlefront on May 9, 1940, facing catastrophe, and again at the side of Schuman and Monnet in the French Foreign Office ten years later. Turning to the new members, so many of whom were his compatriots, he challenged them to assure that there would still be cause for celebration on May 9, 1970.[41]

Little has happened since Poher's speech to reassure him and his friends. On May 15, 1962, four MRP members resigned from the Pompidou cabinet to express their dissatisfaction with General de Gaulle's peculiar vision of Europe. On June 13 of the same year, a large number of deputies walked out of the National Assembly debate on foreign policy for the same reason. "On the same day 293 members of the Assembly, representing all the major political parties except the UNR and the Communist Party, published a statement calling for . . . the merging of the executives of the three Communities, the adoption of majority voting for decisions in all fields in the Council of Ministers, and the direct election of members of the European Parliament."[42]

These events confirm that the European spirit continues to live in France, but that an independent and powerful executive is stifling it. Who will eventually supervene in this clash? Will there still be a

Community in 1970? Will it be international or supranational? Will it still be only a fragment, or a complete political union, and will France continue to participate in whatever survives? These are questions which France's ambivalence has continually raised since 1950, and to which the present provides no unequivocal answer. True to tradition, the struggle for Europe has once more revealed the existence of two French souls. Only this time the division of spirit does not merely threaten the existence of a nation but of an entire continent—and perhaps of a civilization which unlike any other has left its marks everywhere on this globe.

1. For an account of the earliest of these developments consult Elizabeth V. Souleyman, *The Vision of World Peace in Seventeenth and Eighteenth Century France* (New York, 1941); Christian L. Lange, *Histoire du internationalisme*, Vol. I (Oslo, 1919); and Sylvester J. Hemleben, *Plans for World Peace through Six Centuries* (Chicago, 1943).

2. Cf. Anacharsis Cloots, *La République universelle ou adresse aux "tyrannicides"* (Paris, 1792).

3. These remarks are based on Carl H. Pegg, "Der Gedanke der europäischen Einigung während des Ersten Weltkrieges und zu Beginn der zwanziger Jahre," *Europa Archiv*, XXI (1962), 749–58; the same author's "Vorstellungen und Pläne der Befürworter eines europäischen Staatenbundes in den Jahren 1925–30," *ibid.*, XXII (1962), 783–90, and "Die wachsende Bedeutung der europäischen Einigungsbewegung in den zwanziger Jahren," *ibid.*, XXIV (1962), 865–74.

4. Rudolf von Albertini, "Aristide Briand's Union Européenne und der Schuman Plan," *Schweizer Monatshefte*, XXX (1950), 483–91.

5. Marie Granet and Henri Michel, *Combat, Histoire d'un mouvement de résistance de juillet 1940 à juillet 1943* (Paris, 1957), pp. 321–23.

6. Robert d'Harcourt *et al.*, *Dix ans d'efforts pour unir l'Europe, 1945–1955* (Paris, 1956), p. 3.

7. *Ibid.*, p. 6; Richard Mayne, *The Community of Europe* (New York, 1962), p. 80.

8. Kenneth Lindsay, *Toward a European Parliament* (Strasbourg, 1958), p. 38.

9. Mayne, *op. cit.*, p. 81.

10. D'Harcourt, *op. cit.*, pp. 82–83; Mayne, *op. cit.*, p. 99.

11. Bora Ljubisavljevic, *Les Problèmes de la ponderation dans les institutions européennes* (Leyden, 1959), p. 101.

12. The appointments of the Dutch and Luxembourg members reflected the same policy.

13. The fact that Lapie had just lost his seat in parliament and in the Common Assembly would make his appointment all but inexplicable had it not been for his having played a key role in reconciling Socialists and Catholics on the question of public aid to parochial schools. Cf. European Parliamentary Assembly, *Débats*, January 7, 1959, pp. 10–11.

14. For an up-to-date indication of his prominence, see *European Community*, No. 66 (October, 1963), pp. 1–2.

15. Gordon Wright, *Rural Revolution in France: The Peasantry in the Twentieth Century* (Stanford, 1964), p. 169.

16. Mayne, *op. cit.*, p. 112.

17. Cf. Shepard Clough, "Economic Planning in a Capitalist Society: France from Monnet to Hirsch," *Political Science Quarterly*, LXXI (1956), 539–52.

18. Quoted *in extenso* in *L'Europe en Formation*, January-February, 1962, p. 3.

19. Cf. *Débats*, June 26, 1958, p. 405; January 12, 1959, pp. 212–20; and June 25, 1959, pp. 258–59.

20. As a result, there are a number of good studies on the Assembly including P. J. G. Kapteyn, *L'Assemblée Commune de la Communauté Européenne du Charbon et de l'Acier* (Leyden, 1962), and Ernst B. Haas, and Peter H. Merkl, "Parliamentarians against Ministers: The Case of Western European Union," *International Organization*, XIV (1960), 37–59. In the author's analysis of ECSC institutions, *The Path to European Union: From the Marshall Plan to the Common Market* (Baton Rouge, La., 1962), pp. 87–166, the chapter on the Assembly is by far the most detailed. Henry J. Merry, "The European Coal and Steel Community: Operations of the High Authority," *Western Political Quarterly*, VIII (1955), 166–85, has not been succeeded by later and more detailed studies of any of the executive organs.

21. These data are derived from ECSC, *Annuaire-Manuel de l'Assemblée Commune* (Luxembourg, 1956).

22. Until 1962, when the UNR seceded from the Liberal group and formed the only faction in the European Parliament exclusively recruited from one country.

23. Schmitt, *op. cit.*, pp. 146–47.

24. Kapteyn, *op. cit.*, pp. 60–62.

25. Ernst B. Haas, *The Uniting of Europe, 1950–1957* (Stanford, Calif., 1958), p. 424.

26. Kapteyn, *op. cit.*, pp. 194, 194 n.

27. See note 22, *supra*.

28. WEU, Assembly, Second Session, *Document 34: Creation of a Fourth European Assembly* (Strasbourg, 1956), pp. 6–7.

29. *Jahrbuch des Europaeischen Parlaments*, 1961–62, pp. 95–97.

30. *Ibid.*, 1958–59, pp. 90–98; and 1960–61, pp. 100–105, 399–414.

31. Schuman retired from public life at the end of 1962 and died on September 4, 1963.

32. September, 1952–March, 1956.

33. *Débats*, December 16, 1958, pp. 104–5.

34. *Ibid.*, April 13, 1959, pp. 127–36; June 22, 1959, pp. 62–69.

35. *Ibid.*, June 24, 1959, pp. 170–71.

36. For example, see *ibid.*, March 31, 1960, pp. 232–36; April 1, 1960. pp. 276–78.

37. *Ibid.*, March 21, 1958, p. 95.

38. *Ibid.*, November 23, 1959, pp. 89–95.

39. *Ibid.*, November 25, 1959, pp. 258–63.

40. *Ibid.*, March 29, 1960, pp. 84–87; March 31, 1960, pp. 209–11.

41. *Ibid.*, May 10, 1960, pp. 8–9.

42. Michael Palmer, *The Negotiations on Political Union (Planning,* Vol. XXVIII, No. 465 [London, 1962]), pp. 314–15.

Agriculture in France and the European Community   PAUL G. MINNEMAN

IN ORDER TO EXPLAIN the relative position of agriculture in the European Community, it seems wise to describe and interpret some of the forces that have made French agriculture and that of most of Europe what they are today and how these forces are dictating the policy that makes agriculture the most difficult and probably the most critical single problem in the Common Market. After such an exposition it is possible to speculate as to what may happen to agriculture in the Common Market under French hegemony, and how this could affect the United States.

Many attempts have been made during recent centuries to unify Europe, but, until recently, most of these have been by military conquest. The two large countries, France and Germany, frequently have been bitter enemies and each has launched military campaigns to control Europe. After World War I several non-military moves were made toward unification. Only after World War II, however, was a real beginning made in the area of economic integration. After the tremendous destruction of the war, the 1947 Marshall Plan to aid Europe's reconstruction provided the first real catalyst to closer economic co-operation. In that same year, three European nations joined to create a customs union, BeNeLux, and in the next year the foundations of GATT (General Agreement on Trade and Tariffs) were laid; and OEEC (Organization of European Economic Co-operation) was created to help co-ordinate European economic recovery.

In May, 1950, Robert Schuman, foreign minister of France, advocated the pooling of the French and German coal and steel resources because he was convinced that the old trouble areas, the Ruhr and the Saar, needed special attention. Under his guidance, in April, 1951, six countries combined to form the European Coal and Steel Community.

Many people, at that time, also advocated a Green Pool *(pool vert)* for agriculture, but no real progress could be realized toward agreement on agricultural integration. Although work continued on the broader economic problems, it was not until March, 1957, that the Common Market Treaty was signed in Rome. Then, nine months later, it was ratified by the six individual countries and became effective on January 1, 1958. That was nearly seven years ago. The Rome Treaty provided for the gradual establishment, not only of a customs union, but also of an economic union—both of these to be completed over a twelve-year period by 1970.

Several other international organizations, some successful and some unsuccessful, undoubtedly contributed to lay the groundwork for the Common Market (European Economic Community). It appears significant, however, that, whereas the eventual goal of some of the founders of EEC was political unity, only the economic integration has thus far been successful. Schuman publicly recognized the vital necessity for economic unification when he said he wanted to make sure that war between France and Germany "is not only unthinkable but materially impossible."[1]

The first step in creating the Common Market, just as with BeNeLux, was to provide for a customs union of the six members. This provision meant the gradual removal of the tariff barriers between the members and the establishment of a uniform external tariff on imports from third countries. The removal of the tariff walls between the members is a formidable task in itself.

Kings and emperors learned long ago how vital it is to assure an adequte supply of food, especially for national defense in times of war. They sought the maximum degree of food self-sufficiency as an obvious part of national policy. This frequently led to fostering relatively inefficient, high-cost production which had to be protected because it could not compete with the cheaper imports from abroad.

Protection, therefore, has been a cornerstone of European agricultural policy. Germany's protection against imports of cheaper grain dates back eighty years to the age of influential large landholding *Junkers* of Prussia. In fact, self-sufficiency and protection are still the policy today. The memories of food scarceties during the two world wars are still so vivid as to keep this goal an essential part of European agricultural policy. Just before retiring, Chancellor Adenauer stated at a national meeting of farm leaders that food self-sufficiency is good national-defense policy. The French president also declared in August of 1963: "It is not worth talking of a Common Market if it must be understood that Europe is not to obtain its food essentially from its own agriculture which can be largely sufficient."[2]

Another basic objective of policy in Germany, and in France until a few years ago, was to keep the maximum number of persons on farms as a bulwark of both political and economic stability. A large rural population was felt to be essential in order to guarantee an ample supply of food and to provide a source of labor for the city factories and for the armies. This very policy, it appears, has had profound repercussions. It has been primarily responsible for the large number of small farms and, in some regions, the great fragmentation of farms. Of the nine million farms in the six EEC countries, more than five millions, or well over half, have less than twelve acres of crop land. Of Germany's 1.6 million farms, 1.2 million, or three-fourths, have less than twenty-five acres. This is the minimum size the German Ministry of Agriculture considers necessary for a self-sustaining family farm. In France, 55 per cent of the farms have less than twenty-five acres. This has retarded, handicapped, and prevented the development of efficient farming.

These small farms have had to be protected and encouraged by high support prices, which, in turn, were based largely on the higher cost of the inefficient smaller farms. Since farmers were not encouraged to turn to other work, the total income from the available land had to be divided among a larger number of farmers, with the result that the income per farm remained low. More and more government aid and price support became necessary to bolster the income. Thus, the policy of maintaining a large rural population has been responsible for maintaining the relatively inefficient, high-cost production, and for the demands for heavy price support and protection. Not only is such protection achieved by tariffs on imports, but most of the support to European agriculture is accomplished through measures to keep farm prices above the world-market level rather than by tariffs on imports. A recent study[3] by the United States Department of Agriculture shows that 93 per cent of West Germany's agricultural output and 94 per cent of France's are protected by non-tariff barriers, as compared with only 26 per cent in the United States.

Some historians feel that the French Revolution helped to give increased political strength to the farmers, who developed their large numbers into powerful pressure groups to resist displacement and obtain protection.[4] This, in turn, made it possible for the small farmers to preserve their out-of-date agricultural structure and methods. France still had about 23 per cent of her economically employed population in agriculture in 1960, as compared to 14 per cent so employed in West Germany, 8 to 10 per cent in Belgium and the Netherlands, and 8 per cent in the United States. Well over 40 per cent of the total French population is classified as "rural," i.e., living in villages of less than 2,000 inhabitants.

With such a high percentage of the population in agriculture, the farmers wield great political power. One can readily understand why it was necessary in 1957 for the French government to seek the support of its farmers before the Parliament would agree to ratify joining the Common Market. At that time, the French government stressed the idea to its farmers that the Common Market would provide great advantages for French agriculture. French officials pointed out that France still has the greatest potential for increasing her farm production, and that the 170 million EEC consumers would offer French farmers a specially protected market. Although the other member countries expected to gain greater market outlets for their industrial products, France looked to agriculture for her greatest benefits.

It was under these conditions that the Common Market became effective on January 1, 1958. At first, however, its application was limited to industrial products and tariff changes. Not until January, 1962, four years later, could agreement be reached on even the general terms of a Common Agricultural Policy. The extreme difficulty encountered in reaching agreement on agricultural policy is illustrated by the fact that it took 45 meetings lasting 137 hours and 582,000 pages of documents, and 3 heart attacks before agreement was reached on the general terms of agricultural policy.

This policy was described by EEC officials as "the first detailed legislative code on agriculture ever to be adopted by Europe, or for that matter, by any nation." The Rome Treaty listed five objectives[5] of a Common Agricultural Policy (CAP): (1) to increase agricultural production; (2) to insure a fair standard of living for farmers; (3) to stabilize markets; (4) to guarantee regular supplies; and (5) to insure reasonable prices and supplies to consumers.

These objectives are to be achieved in seven and a half years through the use of the following means: establishing common marketing organizations; unifying prices; controlling imports by variable levies; using funds to improve production and marketing, and for export subsidies; and effecting uniform quality standards and sanitary regulations.

Six months after reaching agreement on the general policy, the first variable levies were applied, on July 30, 1962, covering imports of grain, poultry, eggs and pork, and certain standards were applied to fruits, vegetables, and wine. Still under discussion are the proposals for rice, sugar, potatoes, beef, dairy products, and possibly tobacco. No levy procedures are presently contemplated for such products as cotton, soybeans, and tropical products which are not produced in EEC countries.

Basically, the system of variable levies lies at the heart of the program. The objective of the variable levies is to keep the cost of the imported product at least as high as the comparable domestic product. In the case of grain the amount of the levy is the difference between the lowest world-market price and the domestic support price, plus an amount for a preference. Adjustments, of course, are made for quality differences and transportation costs. This concept of variable levies, in place of fixed tariffs, is not new; similar systems had been used previously on grain in Germany and in the Netherlands.

In the case of poultry and other livestock products, the application is somewhat different since these products have no fixed domestic target or support prices. In theory, the levies for these products consist of three parts—an amount equivalent to a duty, plus the amount by which feed and other production costs are higher than in the exporting country, plus an additional amount as preference.

Additional protection is provided against alleged "dumping" by establishing a gate price and by levying a supplemental charge when the c.i.f. price falls below this gate price. Obviously, a great deal depends on the height of the gate price. Originally, it was intended only to prevent imports at dumping prices, but in practice the gate price has been set so high that it results in imposing a supplementary levy. It is very significant that while the import duty on ready-to-cook broilers in Germany was formerly 15 per cent *ad valorem*, the levies during the first half of 1963 were equivalent to about 45 per cent *ad valorem*. This increase has, of course, sharply reduced imports of poultry from the United States.

Another basic and very important concept of CAP is that the support prices are to be made uniform throughout the six countries by 1970. Essentially, the "common" price would constitute a "minimum" price enforced by the variable levies on imports from outside countries. This is especially important in the case of grain since there is now a difference of some 25 per cent between the French price, which is the lowest, and the German, which is the highest. German farmers have been resisting very strenuously any price reduction because it would result in lowering the income which they claim is already too low. They argue that the inflationary process in the other countries will bring their prices up to the German level.

The French government, however, wants to avoid any substantial price increases that would be dangerously inflationary; that would encourage acreage shifts toward sharp increases in grain production; that would result in higher feed costs to livestock producers; and that would make French export surpluses less competitive on the world market. During the past five or six years, the French government has tried hard to hold the inflationary forces in check. As an indication of the importance the government attaches to this, it is worth noting that in October, 1962, retail ceiling prices were reimposed on beef in France.

What can be expected of French agriculture under such a system? What are its potentials? France is the largest and most important agricultural country in Europe. It has the most arable land and the greatest production. It is the largest producer of each of the following products: grain, cattle, meat, poultry, sugar, vegetables, and wine; and is the second largest in potatoes, butter, cheese, and eggs.

In most of these products France now not only enjoys self-sufficiency but has export surpluses. In recent years, its exports of grain have averaged about three million metric tons a year. Only in wine, some fruits, cotton, tobacco, wool, and vegetable oils is France on a substantial net-import basis.

More significant, however, is the fact that French agriculture is the least intensive and therefore still has the greatest expansion potential in the EEC group. There are exceptions to this generalization, such as the fruit, vegetable, and vineyard areas of intensive small farms. In general, however, France still has more good land in ordinary pastures; uses less fertilizer; and feeds her livestock less intensively than the other countries with the exception of Italy. France uses only about 40 per cent as much chemical fertilizer per acre of crop land as Germany and Belgium and only 30 per cent as much as the Netherlands. Her yields of grain per acre and milk per cow average only about 70 per cent of those of Germany, and 55 to 60 per cent of those of Belgium and the Netherlands.

Experts readily agree that French agricultural production will increase substantially, but they do not agree on the extent and rapidity of the increase. Grain production, for instance, may increase in two ways; by a shift to a greater area in grain, or by higher yields per acre. An examination of the trend in yields is revealing.

In spite of a 35 per cent drop in grain acreage since 1900, the total grain production has increased 35 per cent. During the twenty-five years since the beginning of the Second World War, French grain yields have increased 70 per cent, including some shift to higher-yielding kinds of grain, e.g., from rye to wheat, and from oats to barley. In other words, the same thing has been happening in France as in the United States and other countries: agriculture has become much more productive and efficient. It may be assumed that yields will continue to increase at an average rate of 2.5 to 3.0 per cent a year because of the increased use of fertilizer and better varieties and methods. This would normally mean an increase in grain production from about twenty-two million metric tons (average of the past five years) to about twenty-six and a half million by 1970, an increase of four and a half million tons, or about 20 per cent.

The other factor, the possible increase in the area of land devoted to grain, is more problematical. Hasty examination of historical data shows that sixty years ago France had 50 per cent more land in use for the growth of grain than today. Even before the last war she had 20 per cent more than today. That is not to say, of course, that all or even most of the area formerly planted in grain could, or would, be used again for this purpose. Part of the land now serves a non-agricultural purpose, part has become forest and permanent pasture, and part is used for growing fruit and vegetables. Some of the land is, however, used in rotation for pasture and hay, and part of it could undoubtedly be used for grain if higher grain prices offered the necessary incentive of greater net returns.

A recent study by the United States Department of Agriculture reports that the EEC Commission estimates that it is technically possible that a maximum of 1.5 to 1.6 million hectares (3.7 to 3.9 million acres) could be added to the present grain area of France. That would be an area increase of 16 to 17 per cent. Yields on such land would be expected to be lower than on land presently used. Moreover, such a shift could be expected only if grain prices were increased sharply in relation to other prices and the cost of production. This, however, serves to show the tremendous importance of setting the eventual uniform EEC prices for grain at a reasonable level that will not result in distorted shifts toward uneconomic production. EEC is the world's greatest importer of grain; and France is the only one of the six countries that has the potential for increased grain exports. The French minister of agrculture[7] recently stated in Germany that France has thousands of hectares now lying fallow which could be used to produce more grain. "A way must be found," he said, "to compensate German farmers without making us overproduce."

Thus, it seems that various kinds of important pressures for changes are at work both in agriculture and in the economy as a whole. Some of these changes have been under way before EEC, and some are being accelerated by EEC.

The French economy as a whole has made a spectacular comeback during the past five or six years from a dangerously low economic level to general prosperity and stability. France's gross national product has been increasing at the rate of 5.5 per cent a year, nearly double that of the United States. Her gold and dollar reserves now are more than three times those of 1957. The two currency devaluations in 1957 and 1959 made the franc 40 per cent cheaper than it was in early 1957, thus facilitating exports.

While French agriculture, too, has made much progress, it has not kept up with industry. Farmers have complained bitterly and have held widespread public demonstrations. As a result of the former policy of keeping people on the land, French agriculture in 1960 still employed 23 per cent of the total economically employed population; yet they received only 9.4 per cent of the country's gross national product. This shows forcefully the sharp imbalance that exists between per capita income in agriculture and that in the rest of the economy. There are just too many people on the farms and their per capita income is too low. The flow of people from farms to industry is speeding up, but it is not yet fast enough, nor has it been going on long enough to increase materially the size of farms and the income of those who remain on them. The present relatively high rate of industrial activity and the large number of urban job vacancies are stimulating the shift away from agriculture in both France and Germany. Agricultural economists feel that this shift and the resulting structural changes it permits offer the greatest hope for raising the farm income of those who remain farmers.[8]

As French farm output increases, its export surplus problem also will increase. French farmers have been promised great benefits from the Common Market. The minister reminded the public recently that the ratification of the EEC Treaty itself was voted in the French Parliament by the representatives of the farmers. French farmers are politically powerful because they are numerous and well organized. Now, the government is called upon to fulfil its promise by assuring an export outlet in the lucrative German market, which is the most important agricultural import market in the Community.

Since the relatively high costs of production make it impossible for French farmers to compete at world-market prices, they demand preference and protection on the German market to keep out competition from cheaper overseas suppliers. The French minister declared recently: "Opening Europe to free trade in agriculture would be a catastrophe." This French policy goal is clear, and attempts to impose it as the official policy of EEC as a whole are being relentlessly pursued. France is pushing for early completion of Common Agricultural Policy regulations on the products not yet under control. Experience thus far has shown that, once regulations are agreed upon, changes in, or relaxation of, them are almost impossible.

It would seem unfortunate to leave this subject without a brief review of what the Common Agricultural Policy holds for United States agriculture. It is axiomatic that the EEC countries are the world's greatest import market for agricultural products. In 1962, they took over 1.2 billion dollars' worth, or 23 per cent, of American total agricultural exports. For some commodities, this represents a relatively large portion of American production.

Some products, those that are either not produced in the EEC, or only in deficient quantities, are relatively good candidates for export to EEC; for example, cotton, soybeans, oil meal, tallow, hides and skins, and some fruits. For other products, however, the outlook is less favorable because of the higher import duties and levies, and increased domestic production expected as a result of high price supports. These are wheat, rice, tobacco, poultry, pork, dairy products, and some fruits.

To close on a more optimistic note, in so far as United States agriculture is concerned, several possibilities are worth noting. One is that European consumers have not yet had much to say. Prices of some food products have already risen, and if this rise continues, it may arouse wider public opposition to the restrictive measures that reduce imports and raise consumer prices. In most EEC countries, the consumers have to spend 30 to 40 per cent of their income for food, while Americans spend only 19 per cent. The non-agricultural segments of the population, of course, are interested in reducing their cost of living.

Too great a dependence on self-sufficiency and on any one source of supply may also prove to be undesirable. In this connection, it is noteworthy that during four of the past eight years the French wheat crops have been either sharply reduced or damaged as a result of weather conditions.

The array of trade-restrictive measures that have been adopted on agricultural products have been adopted unilaterally; that is, without the agreement or consent of, or any negotiation with, the third countries whose trade is affected. The third countries, therefore, have had no bargaining power when their protests have been disregarded. Unless such restrictions can be made the subject of negotiations, the third countries have no recourse except to take reprisals against EEC. This situation is, of course, unfortunate and may result in trade wars. The better hope is for mutual negotiations in GATT. These should, however, occur before EEC adopts restrictive measures. It is hoped that the so-called Kennedy Round of GATT negotiations in Geneva in 1964 will result in mutually beneficial reductions both in tariff and non-tariff trade barriers.

Perhaps some assurance resides in the old dictum that a country that desires to export must also import. The economies of EEC countries rely on exports and have recently increased their dependence on exports. The oft-repeated EEC claim that it is following an "outward-looking" policy will eventually have to apply to its imports as well as its exports.

1. Walter Hallstein, *United Europe—Challenge and Opportunity* (Brussels, 1962).

2. Statement by President de Gaulle in a press conference, July 29, 1963.

3. "Agricultural Protection by Non-Tariff Barriers," United States Department of Agriculture, *Economic Research Service*, No. 60 (September, 1963).

4. "Agricultural Integration in Western Europe," *Political and Economic Planning* (London, 1963).

5. "Agricultural Policy in the European Economic Community," Supplement to the *Bulletin of the European Community* (Brussels), Vol. V, No. 2 (March, 1962).

6. "France's Key Role in the Grain Sector of the European Common Market," United States Department of Agriculture, *Foreign Agricultural Reports*, No. 122 (April, 1963).

7. Minister Eduard Pisani, Hamburg, September 27, 1963.

8. "Gemeinsames Gutachten," *Report of the Advisory Commission to EEC* (Brussels, 1962).

European Economic Integration in a New Phase   WILLIAM DIEBOLD, JR.

THE TITLE of Nora Beloff's Penguin book on Britain's relations with Europe is *The General Says No*. But what exactly did he say no to? The matter is important because as R. G. Collingwood observed quite a while ago, "you cannot find out what a man means by simply studying his statements. . . . You must also know what the question was" he meant to answer.[1]

Quite obviously, De Gaulle meant that the negotiations under way were to fail, but what else did he mean? Was he making a statement about the conditions under which Britain might enter the Community, thereby leaving open the possibility that they might be met sooner or later? Or was he making a statement about the time at which Britain might enter "Europe"? If so, was he thinking of a few years or, as the language about insularity suggested, a period that would have to be measured in geological time? Or was the main statement not about Britain at all but about the European Community and the changes it would have to make before it could absorb Britain?

Important as these questions are, wisdom cautions against engaging in that fascinating new substitute for the match game—explaining General de Gaulle. The consequences of his statements are of more concern. In politics one answer can dispose of several questions and prevent others from being asked. And answers like the one General de Gaulle gave last January change the next questions.

II

This is not the first time the General has said no to British entry into Europe. While the free trade area negotiations may never have had so good a chance for success as those for British membership in the Common Market, they were still going on in November, 1958, when a unilateral French statement announced that "it was not possible to form a free trade area as wished by the British. . . . " [2] That marked the end of a proposal made by the British but strongly supported by Ludwig Erhard, then the German minister of economics. Washington had sat rather silent but was generally believed to be opposed to the whole idea. There was talk afterward of the "splitting of Europe" and the London *Times* ran a leader called "France the Wrecker." But whatever the merits of the free-trade area would have been—and they might well have been substantial—there was no doubt that ending the negotiations strengthened the Community. The best testimonial to that came in the end from the British when in 1961 they made it clear that they wanted to become members of the Community and suggested it would be possible for them to do things that had been inconceivable before.

It was in a way quite surprising to find De Gaulle in the position of champion of the Community—whatever the reasons may have been that brought him there. Not long before, he had been clearly saying no to the Community. That was during the period of his opposition and virtual retirement. Earlier, in the years just after the end of the war, he seemed to see greater possibilities in some kind of European unity. (Some say that as time passed his gaze shifted from Aix la Chapelle and the throne of Charlemagne westward to Rouen, where in his mind's eye the smoke still rose from Jeanne d'Arc's stake.) It is best, though, not to try to explain these matters, but only to speak of their consequences. When De Gaulle came to power as president of France, no one knew quite what position he would take toward European integration. The likelihood that his attitude would be negative seemed strengthened when he appointed as his first prime minister Michel Debré, one of the very few members of the Common Assembly of the European Coal and Steel Community who was clearly opposed to the whole business. Still, it soon appeared that what De Gaulle was saying about the Community was, in a free translation from the French, "Yes, but. . . ."

He did much more than that. De Gaulle took steps which not only strengthened France in the Community, but also made the Community work better than had seemed likely. The domestic financial reforms and the devaluation of the franc that set the French house in order in 1958 were similar to measures that had been endorsed in one form or another by a series of governments, but it was De Gaulle who put them into effect and made them stick, at least for a period of years. No doubt both this success and the subsequent growth of the French economy owed much to the coming to fruition of investments made over a period of years stretching back to the first Monnet plan.

To appreciate the great importance of the 1958 changes, one must recall how much chronic inflation and balance of payments difficulties contributed to the ambiguity of France's position in the process of western European integration. France was the source of major ideas and policies, but also of reservations and exceptions. She provided a direction and a start and then was often unable to go very far herself. She was frequently both the leader and the slowest vessel in the convoy. France's weakness was the source of a number of escape clauses and delaying mechanisms in the Common Market treaty. The turnabout in France's position (including eventually the Algerian settlement) not only meant that the escape clauses were not used but that the prevailing tone of the French economy had changed from something like fear of the Common Market to confidence and an interest in searching for ways of making the most of new opportunities.

The strong business response—in other countries as well as France—general prosperity, and the improvement in the French position, all helped make possible the acceleration of tariff reduction. Now often taken for granted, this step must stand as one of the crucial events in the history of the Community. The customs union is from two to four years further along than it would have been under the original schedule. More important than the effect of this speedup on trade is the way it convinced people, in and outside Europe, that the Six were really going ahead to form a Common Market, that they would probably move forward on other matters as well as trade, and that they were firmly committed to a new form of intra-European relations. This conviction undoubtedly contributed much to the revolution in British policy toward the Continent. It was also one of the premises of the American ideas about "partnership." Inevitably, the French veto of British entry has raised questions about these policies and the assumption regarding European integration on which they were based. Before examining these questions, however, one must take account of another key element in De Gaulle's policy toward integration.

Monnet, and in somewhat differing ways most other founders of the European Community such as Adenauer, Schuman, and De Gasperi, have always looked toward its culmination in some kind of united Europe. While formulas differed, they all had in common some degree of transcendence of the nation-state. But for De Gaulle, the nation-state is the only real—perhaps the only legitimate— vehicle for political power in the world. Therefore, his vision of a European Community or a united Europe must differ substantially from those of the others. In the short run, the De Gaulle policy emphasizes the organs and processes of intergovernmental co-operation in the Community and tends to depreciate the limited supranational powers and practices that exist in the Community. The problem that this stance poses for the "Europeans"—the advocates of a closer Community—was particularly acute when France proposed new forms of intergovernmental consultation on a wide range of matters. Should one accept something like the Fouchet Plan, as it was called, because the only way to move ahead in European integration was by steps that De Gaulle would take? Or should one refuse in the belief that the French proposal would not only fail to lead to more integration but might weaken the European agencies that already existed? For the British, De Gaulle's emphasis on intergovernmental co-operation seemed to remove one of the main obstacles to their joining the Community since they have never been able to accept the idea of having some supranational body above Parliament. For the smaller countries in the Community, however, De Gaulle's national emphasis seemed to carry the danger of French-German domination. They were inclined to feel that if Europe was to be loosely organized, then Britain should take part in the political discussions. The French and some Germans preferred to move ahead with some kind of political integration before the British had any standing in the process.

Out of this confusion came the French-German treaty of January, 1963, a most important but highly ambiguous event. Was it a substitute for wider political integration or was it intended to force the BeNeLux countries and Italy to agree to something like the Fouchet Plan? Was it essentially a symbolic act marking the degree of Franco-German reconciliation that had been achieved and crowning Adenauer's life work just before he left office? Or was it a very practical understanding designed to insure real co-ordination of policy between the two governments? Was the treaty De Gaulle's effort to perpetuate for France his relation with Adenauer after Adenauer had gone from power? Many Germans now say that it is a symbol of great value with no significant political content. Can they have it both ways? However one looks at the French-German treaty, it is one of the new facts to be taken into account in judging what the next steps in integration are likely to be.

Another new fact is the change of government in Germany. Erhard has never taken the same view of European integration as Adenauer. His dislike of both the Coal and Steel treaty and the Common Market treaty was scarcely concealed. He has always been especially interested in widening the Community. On many matters he would probably oppose tightening the internal bonds of the Community if it limited Germany's freedom of choice in economic policy. There is no reason to believe that he will put as high a premium on agreement with the French as Adenauer did, although for all responsible Germans that must be a major aim. Gerhard

Schroeder also showed signs of diverging from the Adenauer–De Gaulle position even while he was still Adenauer's foreign minister. It does not follow that the past views of these men will persist when they have the full responsibility of governing, but it should at least be evident that there has been a change in Bonn.

There has also been a change in London; but that does not seem of great importance for an appraisal of the present state of integration since it is hard to see what significant initiative in the matter could be taken by Britain. The fact that Britain and Germany will both have elections soon is a fact of somewhat greater potential interest in connection with these problems.

There are other changes too. Some uncertainty about Washington's future policy toward integration is inevitable now that the assumption of British membership in the Community must be, at the very least, suspended. The increased prominence of nuclear issues in transatlantic relations is a reminder that measures of European integration may be chosen on some other basis than a careful balancing of advantages and disadvantages. If the general expectation proves correct that western Europe's economic growth will be slower in the next few years than in the last few, that may also affect the pace of integration. The re-emergence of strong inflationary tendencies in France and Italy is a factor of very considerable importance that could pose a whole new range of questions. Finally, changes in relations between the United States and the U.S.S.R.—for example, more extensive *détente* following the test-ban treaty—could have major effects on the attitude of the chief Continental countries toward integration.

III

This sketch of the changed circumstances in which one must ask what the next stage of economic integration will be points toward a good deal of uncertainty and some generally negative prognoses. To maintain perspective it is worth remembering that if the British had become members of the Community in January, the world would still probably be asking: Will there be more economic integration in Europe soon? What forms will it take?

No matter how much was said about accepting the principles of the Treaty of Rome, and no matter what exactly might have been written down in the protocols of admission, it is inconceivable that a country of Britain's importance could be added to the original Six without significantly changing the Community. This is true whether one is thinking of matters that would have been dealt with in the terms of entry (such as adding to the number of African territories eligible for assocation with the Community), or of the long-range effect on the balance of agricultural interests within the Community, or of the way the Community organs would be altered by the granting of new voting rights and the appearance in Brussels of squads of civil servants from Whitehall. Because they saw these things, many good Europeans who believed that British membership would strengthen the Community in the long run were worried about the effect of British entry on the future of European integration. They felt quite sure that the machinery of the Community would not work as it had been working, especially if several other countries followed Britain into the Community as they were expected to do in the fall of 1962.

It is reasonable to believe that it was largely to meet this problem that the European Economic Commission put forward its Action Program in October, 1962.[3] The Commission wanted to have on the desks of every government and every Community organization an agenda of the unfinished business of integration. The eleven chapters of the Action Program dealt with everything from the elimination of non-tariff trade barriers to adoption of as many common policies as could well be imagined by the end of the transition period. There were concrete suggestions about time tables—stipulating enough work to keep the machine turning over even while it found its new balance, so to speak. Now, in greatly changed circumstances, the same Action Program is still being pushed forward. Every few weeks one or another of its items is taken up for discussion or exhortation. The handling of the issues will surely be different from what it would have been if the British had come in, but the function of the list is oddly similar to what was intended earlier.

The uncertainty of the present phase of integration goes beyond the obvious questions of whether the countries will be able to agree on this or that concrete step. Some of the greatest impacts of the French action have been on the manner in which these things are decided as well as on the process of integration. There was nothing illegal in the French veto since unanimous consent is required to admit new members to the Community. There was also nothing wrong in taking a stiff line in the bargaining and insisting that the British accept this, that, or the other condition without regard to what seemed their special problems. While some of the positions seemed unreasonable, the French often got support from those who were concerned to keep the treaty from being watered down any more than necessary.

Where the French action offended was in its unilateral character and in the unwillingness it exemplified to allow for the possibility that the French position might have to be altered in the end to satisfy not just the British but the other members of the Community. The French action, that is to say, offended against what has come to be regarded as the Community's way of doing things. It is not easy to describe this Community method in a few words, nor does it always manifest itself uniformly. Perhaps its essence is the willingness to work until there is a very wide area of agreement and then to allow the final gap to be bridged either by the use of such supranational powers as are vested in one or another of the Community's organs or by a minority's conceding the last margin for the sake of agreement and progress in the Community. The minority may or may not get an immediate *quid pro quo*, but it does not feel the need to demonstrate that each action in itself bestows national advantages. It can rest its case on the long-range advantages of membership in the Community. This is not the abandonment of national interest, but the reinterpretation of it in a more or less consistent fashion.

102

The French action was a vivid reminder that national political power remains the strongest single force in the Community and that when it is firmly asserted the Community processes at present can not often prevail against it. From the French willingness to take this step every other government in the Community must have drawn certain conclusions regardless of what its leaders felt about the merits of British membership. If France was not going to follow the Community pattern in so fundamental a matter as British membership—presumably just because it was so fundamental—how sure could the others be of what France would do in a wide range of other circumstances? Who could tell when the French might decide that their own compulsions, whether they stemmed from broad historical vision or internal political or economic pressures, would require another assertion of unilateral power? And if one loses the assurance that common decisions will prevail over national actions, then it can easily become important to extract some national advantage as the price of consent at each step.

One hardly needs to trace out this line of thought and the policies to which it would give rise. Does not everyone know about actions that generate equal and opposite reactions? It does not require much imagination to see that almost any government of the Six must conclude that it could not afford to be more heavily committed to an arrangement than the French government was committed and that its hands must be left at least as free as French hands. From this it is only a step to seeing that the process by which decisions are made must also be altered, perhaps subtly. The change will surely be in the direction of giving less weight—though perhaps not very much less—to agreement for the sake of agreement, and of calculating national interests in a more conventional way than that which had been developing in the "Community method." This is not a matter of black and white, of separate national action versus common action, of supranational versus intergovernmental power. These sharp antitheses are unreal so far as the practice of integration is concerned. While that process may not often be very colorful, it is at least in chiaroscuro. It is enough to say that the French action

and the inevitable reaction to it on the part of the other five governments move the Community along the spectrum away from common
action and towards national action and that this is probably the
single most important consequence for European integration of the
French action of January, 1963.

There is some history that is relevant to the new phase of the
problem. A number of features of the Common Market treaty are
very largely the result of concessions made by the other five governments to France. This is true of much of the general language
about harmonization of social conditions and specific provisions
like those concerning equal pay for men and women. The special
trading arrangements for Algeria and Morocco were a concession to
France, and the biggest concession of all was the association of
African territories with the Community. France was essential to the
Community, and her supposed financial and economic weaknesses
provided bargaining strength in getting these concessions along with
the provision for escape clauses. When the situation changed after
1958 and France was strong, she pressed for a common agricultural
policy on the ground that she did not benefit so much as she should
from a common market confined to industrial products. The
Germans felt that the agricultural agreement of January, 1962, had
been to a considerable extent forced on them, and they held back
on its application.

Had Britain entered the Common Market, she might now be
regarded as the cause of some loosening of some Community links.
Some anticipation of that development was probably a factor in the
tendency in some important circles in Germany in the fall of 1962
to approach each item in the Commission's Action Program by
asking, "Is that really something we are required to do under the
treaty?" If the drive for integration were going full steam ahead,
one would have expected the attitude to be, at least more often,
"Is this a good way of achieving the aims of the Treaty? How can
we go about it?" There were, of course, domestic factors encouraging such reticence, just as now the tendency to limit one's commitments in reaction to French policy will be strengthened by other
considerations as well.

How far this loosening will go is a crucial question in connection with the new phase which European integration has entered. It is too soon to find an answer, but one does not have to leave the process to the imagination. One of the first reactions to De Gaulle's veto was the refusal by Italy and the BeNeLux countries to agree to the signing of the new treaty of association with African countries. That proved temporary, and should probably be thought of as a demonstration of pique and frustration rather than a calculation of national advantage. But it was a warning. A subtler, more delayed reaction, is reported by one of the closest American observers of the Community who says, ". . . The day to day work of the Community is increasingly in the Committee of Permanent Representatives [the deputies of the Council of Ministers] rather than by the Commission. . . . " [4] The most important step has been taken, naturally enough, by Germany.

In April, 1963, Foreign Minister Schroeder made some proposals to the Council of Ministers and used a new word to characterize them; "synchronization" promises to take its place in the annals of European co-operation with such other rather fine-sounding but ill-defined terms as "harmonization" and, indeed, "integration" itself. His idea, Schroeder made clear, was that "we should equalize as far as possible the advantages and disadvantages of the measures of the Community as applied to the separate member states. We cannot embark upon a system of advance concessions to be made notably by those countries which have already made considerable concessions up to now." [5] The practical application of the new doctrine was to be a linking of the Common Agricultural Policy with the Community's foreign-trade policy. Germany would agree to further steps to carry out the agricultural policy if France would adopt a position that would permit the Community to offer broad and real tariff concessions on industrial products in the forthcoming tariff negotiations in GATT, "the Kennedy Round." Plainly, this kind of linking will be difficult, since each decision or policy, in fact, comprises many steps over a long period. The Chancellor-to-be Ludwig Erhard may have struck one of the keynotes of the new phase of integration when he told some of the members of his party in Munich that they should not assume that everything is firmly laid down by the Treaty of Rome. "Every day one must think anew about the decisions that are going to have to be taken." [6]

IV

It would be foolish in an essay of this length to try to review all the issues on which the European Community will have to make decisions in the next few years, and unwise, at any length, to try to predict what those decisions will be. But a thumbnail sketch of a few of the major problems may help to give some sense of what may lie ahead.

The Common Agricultural Policy is already a major testing ground of the new phase of integration, and a most difficult one. A few years ago it was reasonable to believe that agriculture might be one of the last major fields in which the Community would achieve common policies. Now, thanks largely to French insistence, it is virtually an article of faith that without a Common Agricultural Policy there can hardly be a Community. This judgment may go too far, but it is clear that the pressures to achieve some kind of agreement are now enormous. This is not the place to discuss the substance of agricultural policies: in another chapter Dr. Minneman has shown how complicated the issues are. It is enough to underline some characteristics of the agricultural problem that make it of special significance to the next phase of integration.

The agreement on a Common Agricultural Policy is a less than wholehearted one. To put it into practice requires a large number of decisions at frequent intervals and the continuous application of complicated regulations. Therefore, it offers a fine collection of opportunities for the playing out of "synchronization" or any other process of national bargaining as a means of integration. Difficult as the problems are, there is almost certainly room for compromise. It follows that agricultural policy will be a good barometer by which to read the course of European integration. Americans, however, must be careful not to confuse the standards by which they judge this process. Closer integration does not necessarily mean a policy that is attractive to outside countries; the opposite is, if anything, more likely. Moreover, the agricultural policies on which the six countries can agree need not be—in fact, are not likely to be—those that contribute most to the economic welfare of the Community.

Energy policy raises quite different issues. Here the countries have as yet no commitments beyond the rather general ones of the Treaty of Rome except with regard to coal (and a certain amount of the difficulty in applying the Schuman Plan treaty arises from the fact that there are no common rules about competing fuels). Several times in the last few years the Community seemed to be on the verge of adopting a common energy policy. Much good exploratory work has been done, and the major alternatives are fairly clear. This clarity is part of the difficulty. Signor Boldrini, the head of Ente Nazionale Idrocarburi (ENI), the Italian government energy agency, says, "The essential objective of a common energy policy is to assure the whole Community a low energy price." M. Maurice-Bokanowski, the French minister of industry, says, "It is inadmissible in the long run to let Europe be dependent for so important a source of energy as oil . . . on the decisions of private companies (which are in fact owned by Anglo-Saxons)."[7] Both views are understandable, but they do not appear to lead in the same direction. The one might be translated to mean that Italy wishes to retain full freedom to buy cheap coal from the United States and cheap oil from the Soviet bloc. The other statement can be read in terms of France's wish to assure markets for her Saharan oil, whether inside the Community or in world markets on a bargaining basis with the large companies. In Germany, strong pressures to take advantage of the cheapness of oil run up against the need to hold the reduction of coal mining and coal miners to politically acceptable levels. Some Germans claim they can take more progressive measures on a national basis than they can under a Community policy under which, for instance, pits might be kept open in Belgium which were less economical than some already closed in the Ruhr.

None of these problems is insoluble, but they suggest that the process of agreeing on a common energy policy requires a strong will to integrate, and one is bound to wonder whether failure to

107

adopt a common energy policy at the height of the wave of integration is likely to be followed by success when integration is less compelling. External pressure has been important in the past; the closing of the Suez Canal and the American rebuff to French and British efforts to seize it gave integration quite a push. The fear that Europe's oil supplies were at the mercy of Middle Eastern governments and the belief that atomic energy would soon become economic did much to make the Euratom treaty more interesting to many people than the Common Market treaty. The premises proved false. Oil is now much more plentiful, west as well as east of Suez. Neither Soviet oil nor Anglo-Saxon oil companies seem, for the time being, to provide the kind of external pressure that might move the Community toward a common energy policy.

The Community's antitrust policy does not raise a question of major new commitments, as energy does, or of continuous national compromises like those in agriculture. In practice, governments will still have to approve some measures, but in the main the problem is one of applying regulations already drawn up and adding new ones to carry out the broad rules laid down in the treaty. There are strong conflicts of interest, but to a very considerable extent they do not run along national lines. One might, therefore, expect that even in a period when countries were not drawing much closer together, there could be progress in these matters. That may well prove to be so, unless governments choose to block action, for instance, by refusing the increased appropriations that would be necessary for a large additional effort. Administration, as Americans should know very well, is the essence of effective antitrust policy. The Community is only at the beginning. At best, progress will be slow.

The longest chapter in the Action Program concerns broad economic policy. Starting with a number of things the six countries already do, it calls for fuller and more systematic comparison of national forecasts and programs, consultation over a wide range of issues, and other steps toward the eventual creation of a Community-wide program that would guide action over a period of years. The Commission proposed to recommend action on concrete problems, such as recession, inflation, and labor shortages, and looked to the time when the six governments would have common or parallel policies concerning economic growth and structural change. The report's language was modest, the approach rather cautious. Nothing very explicit was said about increasing the power of the Commission or even the Council of Ministers in order to make common policies more effective. The word "planning" was avoided. Nevertheless, as was expected, there was a sharp reaction in Germany, especially in the economics ministry, against what was seen as a proposal for some kind of international planning. Of course, Erhard rejects close governmental direction of the economy on any basis, national or international. One suspects that in this case, however, there is also a wish to keep as much freedom of action as possible to meet future German economic problems by measures that seem best to him, whatever foreign officials may think.

Working against these views—which are not so strongly held in the other countries—are the pressures for close co-operation in economic policy that arise from the existence of the customs union. Certainly if there is serious trouble in one or more of the major countries, whether it is inflation, recession, or balance of payments difficulties, there will either have to be agreed action or a severe strain will be put on the Community. It is logical to co-operate on preventive as well as curative action, so one would expect to see some progress along the lines suggested in the Action Program. This is made the more likely by the fact that governments do not have to give up powers to the Commission to co-ordinate their national economic policies.

A similar logic applies to monetary and financial policy. "To coin money, [and] regulate the value thereof" is one of the highest attributes of economic sovereignty, so one might suppose that the shift in emphasis within the Community toward national action would put an end to financial integration. The situation may be almost the opposite. Without hard and fast commitments, with only a few formal procedures, the Six already carry on a high degree of consultation and are generally expected to increase it. This is not a matter of establishing a single currency for Europe, a six-country federal-reserve system, or a pooling of gold or foreign-exchange reserves. It is a question of taking a large number of practical measures made highly desirable by the close links among the six economies. The paradox of achieving an especially high degree of co-operation in most delicate and vital matters but without firm commitment is explained in part by the fact that governments are giving up less freedom of action than may appear, since the discrepancy between the independence of national sovereignty and the actual interdependence of economic systems is particularly marked in these matters.

There are also external factors at work, though how much they do to shape financial and monetary co-operation among the Six is hard to judge. France, Germany, and Italy have for several years been among the principal countries with strong balance of payments positions. As more and more measures of international co-operation prove necessary to strengthen the free world's financial system, questions arise whether the Six should be concerting their policies. Somewhere off in the distance is the possibility of working toward some sort of European reserve currency that might take its place next to the dollar and the pound. The prospects may look very different if French and Italian reserves are rapidly eroded by inflation; but then there will be need for a new kind of common action.

Some observers feel that external relations have very little to do with the financial co-operation among the Six, and that the real driving forces are in the requirements of integration among themselves. It would, for instance, be very disturbing to the customs union if one of its members unexpectedly devalued its currency, or another permitted a high degree of inflation. But is the customs union likely to be completed, or will it, too, be set back by the impact of the French veto on British entry? Few observers seem in much doubt that the Six will go ahead. There may be some slowing-down of the rate at which they remove duties on trade among themselves, either because the remaining 40 per cent of the tariff is the most protective part, or because slower economic growth leads to more frequent use of escape clauses, or because one country or another delays the process as a means of putting pressure on a partner country to act in another sphere. But on balance the evidence seems strong that the combination of commitment, momentum, and advantage virtually assures the completion of the customs union on schedule.

If that is correct, how much further will the Six have to go in integrating their economies? The argument is familiar that one step must lead to another, since a customs union will not work unless countries pursue compatible policies in monetary affairs as well, that it makes no sense to remove tariffs if you permit cartels to regulate trade, that discriminatory transport rates can largely undo the effect of cutting tariffs, and so on. The logic is good, but it is also true that imperfect customs unions are viable and that irrational discrepancies can be tolerated for a surprisingly long time. One should not, therefore, assume that completion of the customs union will guarantee that the Six take other major steps toward economic union. But it will set up significant pressures.

External pressure may also increase the integration of the Six. To take part in the Kennedy Round of tariff negotiations they have to agree on what they will ask from other countries and what they will be prepared to give in return. A whole series of other trade negotiations with, for example, Iran, Israel, and Argentina, also require common action. The need for the Six to deal with the underdeveloped world singly or together poses another series of questions to them, not least because the existing arrangements put the associated African territories in a privileged position which some other outsiders want to share. Thus, circumstances push the Six toward a common commercial policy in spite of the low level of interest in major new measures of integration. To carry out a common commercial policy will probably require agreement on other matters as well. And the birth of "synchronization" shows how the need to agree on foreign-trade policy can provide opportunities for bargaining on the internal affairs of the Community.

V

From this sketch of some of the problems facing the Community can be gathered some idea of the forces making for or working against more integration in the near future. Old forces that have been there all along are also still in operation. The whole familiar case for European economic integration has not lost its validity. Some political and economic groups have acquired a stake in the steps that have already been taken. The familiar obstacles are also still there, whether in the form of private interests or government policies and responsibilities. Groups that once resisted integration may change their positions in an effort to gain from something that is going on anyway; that is largely what happened in the case of French agriculture. With a shadow over the ideal of integration and some clear and present barriers to action, the practical champions of integration may choose to work hard on relatively minor and even technical matters. By doing this, they could hope to make some progress, to keep the wheels turning, and, conceivably, even to set in motion forces that would lead to some broader steps. The existence in the Community organs, and indeed in all the member governments, of a rather large body of people who favor more co-operation and are habituated to formulating solutions in terms of Community interests instead of purely national ones may turn out to be important.

The international political conditions affecting integration are also changed. United States support will probably be more closely linked than before with questions about nuclear strategy. As Professor Brzezinski points out, relations between the United States and the U.S.S.R. could take a turn that would raise new questions in Europe. There is less agreement than before within the Community on the desirability of some form of political integration. There is strong resistance in the five countries to being caught up in De Gaulle's Europe. The wish to keep the door open for Britain will make some of the five governments hesitant to move ahead on a number of matters. It is very difficult, though, to carry on a policy of holding open the door for Britain while at the same time dealing with day-to-day business in the Community, and some erosion of this position may occur.

Old and new pressures can be expected to work rather differently in the Community's new circumstances from the way they did before the French veto. The new emphasis on national interest, limited commitment, and bargaining of a more or less traditional sort seems certain to produce fewer "integrative" solutions to problems than in recent years. Governments will probably find it harder than before to resist domestic interests that oppose specific measures of integration. When the idea of integration flourished, each of the governments could turn in the end to its own people and say, "We must accept less favorable terms than we wanted because otherwise we shall be standing in the way of the development of the Community. By making these sacrifices now we will gain in the end." This will be harder to say in the future; the *quid pro quo* will more often have to be immediately visible and perhaps more closely linked with the concession.

All this plainly adds up to less and slower integration. The dangers of complete breakdown of the process—which were always there—are somewhat heightened, but there is very little evidence that the Community is likely to come apart. To have survived the nine months after the shock of De Gaulle's *non*—or perhaps the first six months were the crucial ones—was in itself a test of strength. It was a period comparable to that after the defeat of the EDC, but there has been no Messina (or Canossa) and there is none in sight. While the Community has proved its survival value as it now stands, its future remains uncertain. Stagnation could, in a year or so, begin to look like breakdown.

Again, the present difficulty must be put in the right perspective, not just that of the rapid progress experienced in the last few years. Flat statements about the Community are no longer adequate; this is a complex organization in which contrary forces are at work. The slowing-down in integration that seems almost certain to come must be contrasted with the speeding-up that took place during the last few years. The Community is ahead of schedule and, in a sense, could afford some delay. If Britain had come in, there would almost surely have been some slowing-down and, undoubtedly, a great increase in uncertainty. Even without Britain, however, the Community would almost inevitably have slowed its pace as it approached economic union. For one thing, the treaty provisions on matters other than trade are mostly rather general and lack precise time-tables. (To supply what was lacking was one of the purposes of the Action Program.) For another, many of the issues raised by the formation of an economic union press more sharply than those of tariff removal or the ultimate responsibility for economic welfare of each government to its own electorate. There are no means in the treaty for rectifying this discrepancy between political responsibility and economic authority; only a major step in political integration could overcome it.

Perspective is also most important in how the new emphasis on national interest and national advantage is judged. When the six governments created the Community, they did not give up the idea of national interest; they reinterpreted it. The process of integration that followed was one in which a mixed political system developed. National political power remained primary, but it was exercised in new ways and in a new setting—and was somewhat altered in the process. Before France vetoed Britain's entry, the conflict of national interest had prevented agreement on a common energy policy; the agreement on a common agricultural policy was a triumph over the traditional calculation of national interest—but a shaky one. What has followed the French veto has been, not the introduction of a new element, but a shift in emphasis—and probably a major one—toward the national way of doing things and away from the Community way.

These reminders are not intended as an optimistic gloss on a gloomy analysis. There has undoubtedly been a setback to integration. But one will fail to understand if everything is explained in terms of a single cause. The new situation is a complex one, and it would be foolish to try to predict what will happen in the next year or two. The European Community has never been very predictable, even when it seemed firmly set in its course. No estimates of its progress made in 1958 were valid in 1960, and certainly most of 1962's forward thinking has proved to have been on the wrong track. It is no easier to judge how each of the members of the Community may calculate its national interest in the new circumstances.

Take France, the subject of this book. What will be France's policy toward integration and toward her partners in the Community during the next few years? Ask the question and a myriad possible answers crowd in, more than can even be catalogued at the end of an essay like this. Few of them concern economic integration alone. Many lead to the conclusion that a resurgence of the old ways of calculating national interest will lead to the loosening of the bonds of the Community. While its complete dissolution seems none too likely, one can easily see how it might come to be a customs union and nothing more. This may well prove to be the case. It is conceivable, though, that France might turn up in the end with a policy aimed at reinvigorating the Community.

Suppose De Gaulle barred Britain because he judged the Community without Britain more suitable to France's purposes (or his conception of Europe, which for the present may be taken to be the same thing). This would imply that France wanted to preserve the Community, in some form and on some terms. That can only be done if the other members are satisfied with what is preserved and what is newly created. The five have shown they are not prepared to break up the Community just because it excludes Britain and even though France infringed the code and acted in a dictatorial manner. How much more will they accept? Probably no one knows, and it would be prudent of the French— always assuming they see some advantage in preserving the Community—to build it up in ways that do not jeopardize what they regard as major national interests.

Germany, Italy, and the Low Countries might think it wise to go along with such a French policy. Their alternatives are limited. Without France they cannot have the kind of European Community they subscribed to when they signed the Treaty of Rome. With De Gaulle's France they cannot have it either. They can go only as far and as fast as De Gaulle will go. To take what they can get of *l'Europe des Etats* will involve doubt, trepidation, and opposition; their policies will have to be based on the kind of bargaining and calculation that underlies "synchronization." If

115

instead they choose no progress over the only kind the French permit, the alternatives for the Community will be rather dreary. They might not, however, be catastrophic. The more radical course of pushing ahead with integration without France is for many reasons an alternative the five seem unlikely to choose. It would reopen all the questions.

If the French decided to try it—and did not miscalculate—they could probably do much to shape the course of European integration for the next few years. That integration would be significantly different from what it has been and probably from that envisaged by most of the architects of the Treaty of Rome. The same sort of result can be expected from almost any other policy France follows short of one that breaks up the Community. To understand this new phase of integration—however long or short its life proves to be—will require continuing reassessment of aims, agenda, and the new processes that are beginning to appear.

1. *Autobiography* (Pelican ed; London, 1929) p. 26.

2. Text in *L'Année Politique*, 1958, p. 482. The statement was made by Jacques Soustelle, who was then still saying yes to the General.

3. *Memorandum of the Commission on the Action Programme of the Community for the Second Stage*, European Economic Community Commission, Brussels, October 24, 1962.

4. Miriam Camps, "Slow Motion in Brussels," *World Today*, November, 1963, pp. 463–68.

5. "What is 'Synchronization'?", *European Community*, June, 1963, p. 4.

6. *Die Welt*, July 8, 1963.

7. Both quotations from Parlement Européen, *Cahiers mensuels de documentation européenne*, July, 1963, pp. 16–17.

France and the Resource Pattern of Western Europe   NORMAN J. G. POUNDS

THE FRENCH HISTORIAN MICHELET once observed that "without a geographical basis, the people, the makers of history, seem to be walking on air, as in those Chinese pictures where the ground is wanting." For many, an understanding of the geographical stage upon which the drama of history and of politics has been played is essential for a proper understanding of the drama itself. In the case of the history of European integration in recent years, stage and drama are inseparable; indeed, the stage is a member of the dramatis personae, and resources and means of transportation have shaped the decisions of the politicians to as great a degree as the politicians have determined the ends to which resources should be put. In this essay, a few of the facets are examined of this interplay of geography, on the one hand, and of history and politics, on the other, as it is demonstrated on the stage of western Europe.

When in 1950 Robert Schuman proposed the creation of a common market in coal and coke and the raw materials and half-finished products of the iron and steel industry, his argument was predicated on contemporary economic conditions. A report of the Economic Commission for Europe,[1] published only a few months earlier, had drawn the attention of the leaders of European industry to the expected consequences of the expansion of steel capacity in the "new" countries. It had recommended improvements in the level of industrial efficiency and specialization and urged that steps be taken "to ensure the free movement from one specialized region to another of the various types of . . . products thus produced."[2]

The warmth with which Schuman's proposals were received and the success with which they were implemented during the following decade were not entirely due to their intrinsic economic merits, great as these were, but owed much to a growing sense of west European unity.

Such a feeling, more often felt than expressed, had helped to shape Western civilization and to give it unity and cohesion. A medieval chronicler spoke of the "seamless web" of medieval Christendom. Toynbee has more recently described[3] how western Europe in the Middle Ages, ringed around by foes, found itself welded into a semblance of unity by the hammer blows of its enemies. This sense of unity, exaggerated as it may have been by the Christian apologists and spanning an area ill-defined but certainly more extensive than that of the present Economic Community, has never entirely disappeared, despite religious and dynastic division.

One must beware of stretching the analogy too far, but there was nevertheless a certain similarity between the position of medieval—especially of early medieval Europe—and that of western Europe in the last fifteen years. During this latter period, the European powers suffered defeat and even humiliation at the hands of their former colonial empires. For the first time, the non-Western world, as it has been somewhat ambiguously called,[4] has seemed not merely hostile—hostility has been an almost normal situation—but also dangerous to the European powers. Their lost empires have in a vague and indefinite way given five out of the six members of the Community, not to mention the United Kingdom, something in common: a feeling of deprivation, of nakedness, and of exposure in a harsh world. It has put them on the defensive. The report of the Economic Commission for Europe, already mentioned, sensed the threat which the new nations were posing to the old established steel industries of Europe. The Latin American nations and those of the Afro-Asian bloc were acquiring in relation to the old nations of western Europe a significance which is more likely to grow than to diminish.

The growth in power and prestige of the Soviet Union, building on foundations laid by tsarist Russia, has, lastly, contributed to this western European feeling of insecurity. In these different ways, the climate of opinion of Europe in 1950 had been made ready to receive the proposals of Robert Schuman, and even to visualize the extension of the scope of the European Community that was defined five years later in the Treaty of Rome.

But however warmly the Community proposals might have been received, they would have been no more effective than the Central American Common Market or a Customs Union in west Africa if western Europe had not offered abundant scope for the kind of integration and rationalization which Robert Schuman and his fellow workers had in mind.

The six countries of the European Community cover together an area of only about 450,690 square miles, less than an eighth of that of the United States, with a total population in 1961 of about 170 millions. The over-all density is high—about 146 per square

TABLE 1

LAND AREA, POPULATION, POPULATION
DENSITY, AND THE LABOR FORCE
IN EEC NATIONS

	Area in Square Kilometers	Population, 1961	Density per Square Kilometer	Percentage of Labor Force in Agriculture, 1960	Percentage in Mining and Manufacturing Industry, 1960
France	551,208	45,960	83	23	28
Belgium	30,507	9,184	301	8	38
Luxembourg	2,586	317	123	21	*
Netherlands	33,612	11,637	346	10	32
West Germany ..	248,454	54,027	217	14	48
Italy	301,225	49,455	164	31	31
Total	1,167,592	170,580	146	20	*
U. S. A.	9,363,389	183,742	20	7	23

* No data available.

mile; highest in the Netherlands with 900; lowest in France with 22. The region is highly urbanized and industrialized. In no state, except Italy, is more than 25 per cent of the population dependent upon agriculture, and all must be regarded as primarily industrial countries.

These crude data, when compared with the corresponding figures for the United States, indicate a population of similar size in a very much smaller area, a much larger employment in agriculture, and a smaller employment in manufacturing. The primary point of contrast from the geographical point of view is a certain narrowness in the range of physical environments in the Community countries. For geographical reasons, it would be difficult for them ever to have the range and variety of production which characterize the United States. The higher employment in agriculture suggests a lower level of technology and, thus, a smaller per capita income. Although their combined population falls very little short of that of the United States, both their production rate and domestic market potential, as suggested by their combined gross national products, are considerably less.

The Community countries as a whole have a strong and varied relief. In all of them there are extensive areas of land unfit for cultivation and even for grazing. In many places, the climate does not favor crop-farming, and everywhere arable land, won from the forest and waste with difficulty, is maintained in good condition only by continuous effort.

In few other natural resources is the endowment generous. The non-ferrous metals, never really important, are now obtained within the Communty countries in only very small quantities. Petroleum and natural gas have been discovered in recent years, especially in southwestern France, in northern Germany, and in neighboring areas of the Netherlands, but their production remains wholly inadequate for the needs of the Community (see Table 2).

The only mineral resources of major importance are coal and iron ore; and their distribution, exploitation, and consumption will be discussed below. Western Europe has, however, another and unique resource in its rivers. As potential sources of power they

TABLE 2

PETROLEUM PRODUCED IN AND
IMPORTED BY NATIONS IN
THE EEC (1961)

	Petroleum Produced*	Petroleum Imported*	Natural Gas Produced†
France	2,164	39,683.0	4,013
West Germany	6,205	42,303.5	927
Italy	1,971	37,652.1	6,863
Netherlands	2,046	29,427.9	488
Belgium and Luxembourg	....	14,322.8	....

* In thousand metric tons.
† In millions of cubic meters.

may not rate highly, but their regularity and reliability, their geographical relationship to physical resources, and the relative ease with which they can be interconnected by canals gives them an important role in the transportation system of western Europe.

In the following pages, these general remarks on the agricultural, fuel, and mineral resources of western Europe and on its pattern of waterborne transportation will be amplified; and the attempt will be made to demonstrate the role which they are now playing in the closer association of France with her neighbors in the European Community.

The legend that the countries of western Europe were primarily engaged in trading their manufactured goods with distant producers of food stuffs and raw materials is rapidly losing what little truth it may once have had as these other countries themselves gradually became industrialized. The west European countries are, in fact, one another's best markets. Table 3 shows that a growing proportion—in 1961, 37 per cent—of the total foreign trade of the countries of the Economic Community has been with one another, while commerce with the United States, as a percentage of the whole, has ranged between 6 and 9 per cent of the Community's exports. Imports from the United States have been consistently

TABLE 3

Foreign Trade of Nations in the EEC

	Exports of EEC Countries					Imports of EEC Countries				
	Total	To U.S.A.		To Other EEC Countries		Total	Per Cent From Other EEC Countries	From U.S.A.		
		Total	Per Cent	Total	Per Cent			Total	As Per Cent of U.S. Exports	As Per Cent of EEC Imports
1961	32,320	2,240	6	11,900	37	32,170	37	3,502	17	10
1960	29,730	2,240	7	10,250	34	29,590	34	3,420	17	12
1959	25,230	2,380	9	8,170	32	24,310	33	2,370	13	10
1958	22,770	1,670	7	6,860	30	22,940	30	2,400	14	11
1957	22,470	1,500	6	7,160	32	24,820	29	3,170	15	13
1956	20,070	1,410	7	6,430	32	22,350	29	2,860	15	13
1955	18,370	1,160	6	5,650	31	19,280	29	2,100	14	11
1954	15,780	930	6	4,650	29	16,620	28	1,810	12	11
1953	14,090	1,030	7	4,010	28	14,920	27	1,460	9	10
1952	13,770	870	6	3,680	27	15,140	24	1,770	12	12
1948	6,500	325	5	1,700	26	10,470	16	2,480	20	24

larger, ranging from 10 to 24 per cent of the total Community imports and rising in recent years to 17 per cent of the total United States exports. Clearly, the United States could be hurt very seriously if, as is to be expected, the volume of intra-Community trade increases at the expense of that between the Community and other countries.

The next table shows the proportion which manufactured goods has borne to the total EEC trade (see Table 4). Even more interesting than the considerable export of agricultural produce by most of the Community countries is the import of manufactured goods. In these facts lie both the potential and the significance of the Common Market.

The six countries of the Common Market are small in area and extend over a restricted range of environments, and each member has thus a limited range of natural resources. In the past, they impinged on one another's interest as they struggled for resources and services which each thought desirable or necessary. Their interlocking boundaries, their restricted access to good harbors, their unwillingness to place any great reliance on one another for the supply of essential commodities have all shown how inter-dependent these countries had really become, despite their not infrequent hostility, during the period of industrial development of the last two centuries, and also how great would be the advantages of closer association with one another.

Agricultural resources. The smallness of western Europe and its limited range of climate have made it inevitable that agricultural production should in general be parallel rather than complementary within each of the Six. One would, in fact, expect their exchange of goods to be on a relatively small scale, yet even in this field the volume of trade within the Six is large and growing, and De Gaulle is able to speak, even if somewhat unrealistically, of the potential self-sufficiency of the Community in the products of temperate agriculture.

The cost of agricultural production in each member state is conditioned both by the natural or physical conditions under which it is carried on and by the social structure in which it is practiced.

TABLE 4

IMPORTS AND EXPORTS BY EEC NATIONS, BY COMMODITY (1961)

	PERCENTAGES OF EXPORTS				
	Belgium and Luxembourg	France	West Germany	Italy	Netherlands
1. Food and live animals	5.0	12.0	1.0	13.0	24.0
2. Beverages and tobacco ...	0.5	4.0	0.5	2.0	1.0
3. Crude materials	8.0	8.0	3.0	4.0	8.0
4. Mineral fuels	5.0	4.0	6.0	5.0	13.0
5. Animal and vegetable fat and oil	0.5	1.0	0.5	0.5	1.0
6. Chemicals	6.0	9.0	11.0	8.0	9.0
7. Manufactured goods	53.0	30.0	24.0	23.0	19.0
8. Machinery	15.0	24.0	45.0	30.0	19.0
9. Miscellaneous manufactures	6.0	8.0	8.0	14.0	5.0
10. Others	1.0	...	1.0	0.5	1.0
Total agricultural (1, 2, 5) .	6.0	17.0	2.0	15.5	26.0
Total manufactures (6, 7, 8, 9)	80.0	71.0	88.0	75.0	52.0
Total exports (in millions)	196,219.7 Fr.	35,586.7 NF	12,687.2 US$	2,617,346 Lire	15,712.3 Gu.

TABLE 4—Continued

		PERCENTAGES OF IMPORTS			
	Belgium and Luxembourg	France	West Germany	Italy	Netherlands
1. Food and live animals	11.0	14.0	22.0	14.0	11.0
2. Beverages and tobacco	2.0	5.0	2.0	2.0	2.0
3. Crude materials	15.0	22.0	21.0	4.0	12.0
4. Mineral fuels	10.0	17.0	8.0	5.0	13.0
5. Animal and vegetable fat and oil	1.0	1.0	2.0	0.5	1.0
6. Chemicals	7.0	6.0	4.0	8.0	6.0
7. Manufactured goods	24.0	16.0	22.0	23.0	22.0
8. Machinery	22.0	16.0	11.0	30.0	25.0
9. Miscellaneous manufactures	7.0	3.0	4.0	13.0	6.0
10. Others	1.0	...	4.0	0.5	2.0
Total agricultural (1, 2, 5)	14.0	20.0	26.0	16.5	14.0
Total manufactures (6, 7, 8, 9)	60.0	41.0	41.0	74.0	59.0
Total imports (in millions)	210,951.7 Fr.	32,959.7 NF	10,940.9 US$	3,264,024 Lire	18,651.5 Gu.

The former can be modified to only a small degree; the latter is capable of being revolutionized within a relatively short period of time.

The pattern of land use is broadly similar in all countries of the Community. Each has a considerable area of land unfit for agricultural use, given over to rough grazing or forest. In all of them, except Italy, pasture and meadow cover a considerable area, a concession to the cool and damp climate. The following table gives the proportions of the total land area of each of the six countries under the four major categories of land use (see Table 5).

It is difficult to make precise comparisons of physical advantages and of social organization among the six members of the Community, for these are relative and subjective. It may be suggested, however, that in terms of physical advantages France ranks high and perhaps first, and that French agriculture in its social organization has in very recent years moved from a relatively low position almost to the head of the table. In discussing France's relations with fellow members of the Community, one cannot ignore her relatively large agricultural resources and the ways in which they have been used in recent years.

The fact is that two countries within the Community—France and the Netherlands—and at least one outside it, Denmark, have large

TABLE 5

Land Use in EEC Nations (1961)

	Land Area (in Square Kilometers)	Percentage under			
		Arable	Meadow and Pasture	Forest	Other
Belgium	30,510	31	25	19	25
France	551,210	39	24	21	16
West Germany	242,780	35	23	29	13
Italy	294,010	54	17	20	9
Luxembourg	2,580	30	25	33	12
Netherlands	32,450	32	39	8	21

and important agricultural surpluses for export. The Dutch performed in the nineteenth century the tasks which the European Economic Commission's report on steel urged heavy industry to do in the mid-twentieth; they specialized in the crops—mainly fodder and pasture—for which their damp polders were most suited, and equipped themselves to become a significant exporter of dairy and related produce. French agriculture remained, with certain significant exceptions, almost medieval until the twentieth century. In recent years, however, it has undergone a revolution, and its farms, their fields partially rearranged and their methods half-mechanized, are now among the most productive in Europe. France has not only a larger proportion of her area under crops than any other member of the Community, but she has a higher proportion of good quality soil and a much lower density both of rural and total population. Even before this agricultural revolution had made significant progress, France could in a good season break even in the supply of bread crops. Now there is an embarrassingly large export surplus.

All other members of the Community are net importers of wheat, and the West German shortage is a relatively large one. In each of them, the area under bread crops is either restricted by the harshness of the north European climate or, as in Italy, by poor soil and rough terrain. And in each, the crude density of population is greater than in France and the proportion engaged in non-agricultural pursuits is, except in Italy, higher. In Germany, Belgium, and Italy, the competitive disadvantages which result from the environment are intensified by the man-made structure of agriculture: small and highly fragmented farms and a relative lack of capital. Limitations of space prevent a discussion of the differing commercial policies pursued in the nineteenth and early twentieth centuries that have produced these contrasts. In all those countries which today have a weak agricultural structure farming was highly protected, whether for reasons of nationalism or nostalgia.

The contrasts between the present structure of agriculture in France and perhaps also in the Netherlands, on the one hand, and in the other members of the Community, on the other, may be expected to diminish as the "Green Plans" and other devices for updating agriculture achieve their objectives. In the meantime, France, under Common Market conditions, can expect to enjoy a large market for food surpluses—of which wheat is only an example —in most other countries of the Community.

Efficient as French agriculture is by European standards, in many respects its costs of production are higher than those in Canada, the United States, and other more recently developed countries. A relatively low target price for wheat within the Community would be likely in the long run to favor French exports to Community countries. Import levies would raise the price of wheat from any non-Community source that might be cheaper to the level of the target price and thus would, in the long run, exclude it except under abnormal conditions. This particular pricing system has recently been instrumental in raising the price of chicken meat imported into the Community. It is thus inevitable that France, in particular, and, to a certain extent, other members of the Community should do all in their power to exclude farm produce from the United States, the Commonwealth, and other sources where, for geographical or social reasons, it can be produced more cheaply than in western Europe.

French agriculture is more efficient in more ways than that of other members of the Community. But most of them have developed agricultural specializations, such as Dutch dairy produce, Italian fruit and vegetables, and the vintages of Germany and Italy, which can nevertheless command a market in other countries of the Community. The effect of the Common Agricultural Policy will be to insure the expansion of this market by protecting these specialities from competition from outside the Community by means of import levies.

Mineral fuels. With the development of industry in the eighteenth century, these acquired an importance no less than that of agricultural resources. They are, furthermore, highly localized, and no amount of ingenuity can beneficiate really low-grade deposits or develop mines in areas not naturally endowed with minerals.

Coal was the basis on which the industrial structure of western Europe was built. This region is comparatively well endowed and is estimated to contain about 43 per cent of the proven reserves in Europe west of the Ural Mountains. But coal is not a simple, uniform commodity. The qualities of coal differ so greatly among themselves that they are, for practical purposes, different commodities. Anthracite, gas coal, flame coal, and coking coal have, under modern technological conditions, uses so narrowly defined that they can no longer be substituted for one another as was possible at one time. Another important consideration is that the optimum size of a coal mine—or of any other mine—has increased sharply since the nineteenth century. Small coal mines are not competitive, and this means, in effect, that small coal deposits are of necessity abandoned and that mining is increasingly concentrated on the larger.

France is notable for the very large number of small coal basins, which in the eighteenth and nineteenth centuries supplied the demands of their local regions. Distance protected many of them at that time from the competition of larger and more easily exploited fields. But during the nineteenth and early twentieth centuries the smaller fields were one by one obliged to close, and railroads and, to a smaller extent, rivers and canals were used to transport coal from more distant sources. France became a heavy net importer of coal, much of it from Great Britain, and there was a tendency for the iron smelting industry—a heavy consumer of coal—to move to the coast.[5] It is interesting to note that the abandonment of mining in the small coalfields, which are particularly numerous in central and southern France, led to a weakening of the position of the specialized manufacturing industries—generally metallurgical—that had been based on them. The Monnet Plan and the Economic Community are together giving the coup de grâce to many of these small industrial centers.

In 1878, the German government instituted an inquiry into the cost of iron manufacture.[6] One of its witnesses, an ironmaster from Saarbrucken, in commenting on the competitive position of the iron-smelting industry of the present Saarland, remarked that the quality of Saar coal was such that it yielded only a soft, friable coke unsuited for use in such large blast furnaces as were then being built in Great Britain and the Ruhr. He had, in consequence, to face the disadvantages that resulted from the employment of low furnaces. The fact is that for almost a century now the coal of the Saar coalfield has provided an unsuitable blast-furnace fuel—a fact which was either unknown or happily ignored by Clemenceau and the French when they presented their claims on the Saar Territory in 1918.

TABLE 6

Coal Resources of EEC Nations

	Total Probable Hard-Coal Reserves*	Probable Reserves of Coking Coal Included in Column 1*	Production in 1961†
France	9,924	1,004	52,358
Luxembourg	...	...	...
Belgium	11,000	3,780	21,539
Netherlands	4,402	2,100	12,621
West Germany	224,553	148,200	143,615
Ruhr coal field ...	213,600	145,000	120,000‡
Italy	24		741

* In millions of metric tons.
† In thousands of metric tons.
‡ An approximate figure.

Coal resources are distributed very unevenly throughout the Community countries (see Table 6). Luxembourg has none and is wholly dependent upon imports for the supply of mineral fuel. A coalfield stretches from east to west across northwestern Europe from the southern extremity of the Netherlands, or Limburg, through central Belgium into northern France. At its eastern extremity near Aachen it extends into West Germany. Despite considerable disadvantages— the extreme folding and faulting, the thinness of the coal seams, and their high gas content—this coalfield, or at least its eastern extremity, was opened up in the Middle Ages and became in the eighteenth century, as mining spread westward along it, perhaps the most intensively exploited in Europe. It is more generously endowed than most of the coalfields of France, but its coking coal is small in quantity and of indifferent quality. The Belgian section of this coalfield was the scene of an intensive industrial development in the early nineteenth century, and its resources have been depleted. The mines are old, costly to operate, and, judged by the frequency of severe accidents, dangerous. At present, marginal mines are being closed, and, though new mines have been sunk to the north in the newly opened Kempenland field, Belgium remains a small net importer of coal.

The same is true of the Netherlands and Italy, both of which have a coal production which is quite inadequate to supply local demands. Germany, on the other hand, is endowed with the richest European coalfield in terms of both the variety and the amount of coal. Most of this immense reserve, amounting to about 35 per cent of Europe's total resources, is in the Ruhr coalfield. By contrast with the small, contorted fields of the other members of the Community, the Ruhr deposits are thick, free of major geological disturbances, easily worked, and varied in their chemical and physical compositions. The Ruhr coalfield is now capable of supplying the needs of much of western Europe at a delivered price lower than that of local fuel; and in consequence of this, much of the continent, including parts of France, has come to depend upon the Ruhr for at least a supplementary supply of coal. It might almost be said that the Ruhr coal producers, which until the Allied decartelization policy included most of the iron and steel concerns, were in a position to blackmail half the continent. And it was just this, as industrial and commercial interests in Lorraine have repeatedly claimed, that the Germans did. The whole of western Europe is in some degree dependent upon the Ruhr, especially for its supply of coal of coking quality. It is an ironic comment on the French claims to the Saar Territory that its coal proved not to be usable in the French iron industry without an admixture of coal from the Ruhr.

The creation of the European Coal and Steel Community insured at least that the French iron industry would have unrestricted access to the coal resources of the Ruhr, and that no impediments would be placed in the way of purchasing it in the open market. At the same time the over-all dependence of France has been reduced in part by the opening up of the deep extension of the Saar coalfield into northern Lorraine, in part by the development of new methods of blending coals for the coking furnace.

Iron ore. It is impossible to divorce the discussion of the use of Ruhr coal from that of Lorraine iron ore. The minette deposits of eastern France are a low grade deposit of immense extent. They are easily mined; in part they are self-fluxing, and their location is convenient to rail and water transportation. Their total metal content is estimated to amount to about 22 per cent of that of all European reserves. There are, in fact, no other large deposits within the area of the Community, though small deposits, some of them of high quality, continue to be worked. The Lorraine ores were of little importance before the late nineteenth century, primarily because of their low metal and high phosphorus content. In fact, metal smelted from them proved to be unusable by the Bessemer or acid process. Their real value was appreciated only after the discovery in 1879 of the basic or Gilchrist-Thomas process of steel-making. Since that date, about a billion tons of ore (iron content) have been taken from the minette deposits of eastern France and neighboring Luxembourg. This growth came at a time when the iron and steel industries of the Saar valley and the Ruhr were developing rapidly. Lorraine supplied most of the ore used in the Saar which, at its nearest point, is only about thirty miles from the ore deposits. The volume of ore which went to feed the far larger and more numerous furnaces of the Ruhr was, however, very small throughout this period.

There were good reasons for this. The iron-ore field was at this time divided by the Franco-German boundary. The French opened up their sector and, with the aid of both local and German fuel, established a smelting industry at such centers as Nancy, Pout-à-Mousson, and Longwy. The Germans similarly developed the more easterly sector of the iron-ore field with aid of coal or coke transported by rail from the Ruhr. Crude steel and "semis" were shipped, also by rail, to fabricating industries throughout western Germany.

This arrangement seemed reasonable in view of the low metal content of the ore, which rarely exceeded 30 per cent, and the consequent high transportation costs for the ore itself. With a steadily improving iron-coal ratio, moreover, it was more economical to take fuel to Lorraine than to convey Lorraine ore to the Ruhr coalfield by rail. On the other hand, this pattern could have been radically changed if the river Moselle, which rises in eastern France, traverses Lorraine, and cuts across the Rhineland plateau in a series of incised meanders to join the Rhine at Coblenz, could have been made navigable for barges throughout its length. The canalization of the Moselle had been proposed and plans prepared as early as the 1880's. It ran, however, into vigorous opposition from the German side, and this resistance was intensified after the whole of Lorraine had been reunified in French possession at the end of the First World War. The German argument may be summarized thus: The Ruhr industry had equipped itself to use ores from other sources, notably Sweden. Furnace design and equipment for handling ore, fuel, flux, metal, and slag had all been adjusted to a quality and grade of ore that were superior to those of Lorraine. Once established, it was technically difficult to make any major change in the pattern of ore supply, as was demonstrated during the Second World War when the Ruhr ironmasters were obliged in part to substitute Lorraine for Swedish ores. This upset the balance of their operations so seriously that part of the Rheinhausen plant, for example, had to be closed. Another objection to the opening up of the Moselle for navigation was that fuel would become so cheap to the Lorraine ironmasters that they would be able to undersell those of the Ruhr. Furthermore, it was argued, the Moselle was already canalized within France, and the cost of future work on the river would fall upon Germany while the advantages would accrue mainly to France. Add to this that during the period between the two world wars neither France nor Germany had any desire either to assist or to become dependent on the other to any greater degree than was necessary, and it becomes obvious why it was necessary to wait until 1956 for a Franco-German agreement to make the Moselle navigable from Lorraine to the Rhine. The West German government undertook to regulate the Moselle, and France in return retroceded the Saar Territory, which became the tenth *Land* of the Federal Republic. Work was begun on the dams and sluices almost at once, and it is expected that it will be finished by the end of this year and that the movement of fuel and ore by barge will begin at once.[7] Luxembourg has ceased to be an exporter of ore, but depends mainly on the Ruhr for her fuel supply, and is also likely to benefit from the opening up of the Moselle river to navigation.

This is, of course, a very important step toward closer integration of at least heavy industries in the three countries. The advantage to Lorraine, and to some extent also to Luxembourg and the Saar, is likely to be felt at once as freight charges on coal and coke are reduced. The effect on the Ruhr is more likely to be delayed for the reason, already mentioned, that a change in ore supply cannot be effected without in some degree retooling the industry.

It is manifest, however, that the Ruhr-Lorraine-Luxembourg axis, though it may dominate the iron and steel industry of Europe, by no means controls it. About a tenth of the steel made comes from the Belgian centers of Liège and Charleroi, where local fuel is used to smelt ore from both Lorraine and sources outside the Community. During the present century, the dependence on sources of ore outside western Europe has led to the more frequent building of smelting and steel works at the ports in order to avoid the costly transshipment of ore. All Italy's integrated iron and steel works are now at coast sites, such as Genoa and Naples. The only Dutch works is on the coast at Imuiden, and both France and West Germany are in the process of developing coastal locations, such as Dunkirk and Bremen. This clearly denotes a tendency to look away from west European sources of ore, and reflects the relatively high cost of the land transportation of Lorraine ore. It also anticipates a growing export market for steel goods. This tendency for iron and steel works to move to the coast has been present for almost a century, and it is too early to say whether the new Moselle waterway will modify significantly the relative importance of coastal, as against inland, locations for the iron and steel industry.

Inland navigation. Closely related to developments along the Moselle and to industry in the Ruhr and Lorraine is the question of transportation by water in northwestern Europe. The Rhine, navigable for large river barges from Basel in Switzerland to the sea, is the most intensively used waterway in the world. It borders or crosses France, Germany, and the Netherlands; its navigable tributaries link it with Belgium and Luxembourg; and linking canals spread out over the whole area of the Community excepting only Italy.

Since the Middle Ages commerce has converged on the ports of the Rhine mouth, and, as the Rhine itself splits up into several distributaries, the number of ports which may be said to serve the river is considerable. Within the deltaic region of the Rhine mouth are two of the leading ports of the continent, Rotterdam and Antwerp. To the northeast is Amsterdam; to the southwest, Dunkirk—both linked by canal with the Rhine and also serving in some degree as Rhineland ports. More remote, but competing nevertheless with the Rhine-mouth ports, are Le Havre, Emden, Bremen, Bremerhaven, Hamburg, and the Elbe ports. The hinterlands of each of these ports extend into the heart of the continent, and the complexity of the internal transportation nets has made it inevitable that these hinterlands should overlap and compete. To the inevitable pressure of the administrative authorities in each port for the extension of its service area, there has in the past been added the concern of governments that essential services not be under the control of a foreign power. Given the relative cheapness of the transportation of bulk goods by water, it was inevitable that the Rhine-mouth ports would tend to handle the lion's share of the seaborne commerce of northwest Europe. It was no less inevitable that France and Germany would do what they could to divert traffic from the Rhine-mouth ports which lie in Belgium and the Netherlands to their own. What might not so readily have been anticipated was that there should be an intense rivalry between the ports themselves within the area of the Rhine delta.

The result was an overextension of port facilities and the construction of canals for the primary purpose of enhancing the competitive position of certain ports. Thus, the Dortmund-Ems canal was cut to divert to the port of Emden part of the Ruhr's traffic in iron ore and coal that could equally well have been handled by

135

Rotterdam. Similarly, the French port of Dunkirk has been put into such intimate relationships with the industrial region of northern France that traffic has been diverted to it from the ports of Ghent and Antwerp. Above all, the rivalry of Antwerp and Rotterdam has in the past been exceptionally bitter. The diseconomies of this situation may not be calculable, but are nonetheless obvious. The implementation of the Treaty of Rome and of agreements such as the Franco-German treaty of October, 1956, is likely to alter significantly the commercial pattern of northwest Europe. The immediate effect is likely to be to concentrate more foreign trade in the Rhine-mouth ports. One may hazard the guess that the northwest German ports may suffer somewhat, though their loss of traffic is likely to be disguised by the general rise in total trade. There are indications also that the French Rhine ports, especially Strasbourg, will increase their commerce as the economies of river transport to the Rhine mouth over the rail haul to the Channel ports becomes apparent.

The port of Hamburg had, before the division of Germany, served a hinterland which embraced much of the present East Germany and Czechoslovakia by way of the canalized Elbe. Much of Hamburg's former hinterland is now cut off by the zonal boundary, and the port now serves part of West Germany, though waterborne transportation necessarily plays a very much smaller role in the present trade pattern than it did formerly. Present German plans include the construction of branch canals from the Mittelland waterway to Hamburg.

The improvement and extension of the north German waterways will make the northwest German ports more effective competitors with the Rhine-mouth ports and will allow them to serve more directly the commercial needs of the Ruhr industrial area. Nevertheless, the removal of artificial restrictions and restraints on trade can be expected only to increase the importance of the Rhine-mouth ports, and the expansion of their commerce has been anticipated by the construction of a new port, known as Europort, near the New Waterway, west of Rotterdam, for handling specialized bulk commodities. In so far as France is concerned, one may anticipate a larger French fleet of Rhine barges, greater activity in the French river and canal ports of Kehl, Strasbourg, and Mulhouse, improvements along the feeder waterways, notably the Rhine-Marne canal and the Saar Coal Canal, and the improvement of navigable connections between the Rhine and the Saône-Rhone system.

Pipelines. Another aspect of the integration of transportation systems within the Community is the construction of petroleum pipelines. The great complexity and high cost of the terminal installations have limited their number to only a few ports, and fortunately this development came after the formation of the Community had made possible a rational selection of ports to be developed in this way. In short, there are now five major ports handling the import of petroleum and crude oil in continental western Europe, each linked by pipeline with the more important consuming centers. Four of these, Rotterdam and Wilhelmshaven in the north and Marseille and Genoa in the south, are of international importance. Pipelines from refineries at Genoa will supply northern Italy and, by way of a tunnel under the Alps, part of Switzerland as well. Another pipeline is being built from Marseille up the Rhone and Saône valleys to the Rhine at Strasbourg, where it will connect with a pipeline from Cologne. At its northern end, this pipeline system will be fed by pipelines extending inland from the North Sea ports of Rotterdam and Wilhelmshaven. Refineries have been completed or are under construction in the Ruhr area and near Karlsruhe and Strasbourg.

In time, the use of pipelines will influence the traffic pattern on rivers and canals, part of which is made up of petroleum barges. Already, shipping on the Rhine is feeling this competition. At the same time, however, a flexible pattern of water transportation is being replaced by an inflexible pattern of pipelines, the high cost of which is likely to insure that they are utilized as fully as possible. The pattern of pipelines can, of course, be extended, but the investment in it and in its auxilliary refineries makes it unlikely that it will be readily changed or replaced by any different method of distribution. Commercial agreements can be changed or broken with fluctuations in policy, but the amount of "fixed hardware" that is now being created will make it extremely difficult technically to reverse the present trend toward integration in western Europe.

In the past, one spoke of an industrial axis extending from northern France across Belgium and north Germany to Poland, following broadly the belt of coalfields. This is being replaced by a Rhineland industrial axis, spread about the Rhine and its navigable tributaries, with petroleum pipelines and refineries and nuclear-powered generators and their transmission lines for additional stiffening. This new axis, spreading as it does across the boundary of France and Germany and linking together the resources of both, is a hostage for their future collaboration.

1. *European Steel Trends in the Setting of the World Market* (Geneva: Steel Division of the United Nations Economic Commission for Europe, 1949).

2. *Ibid.*, p. 93.

3. Arnold J. Toynbee, *The World and the West* (New York, 1957).

4. Vera M. Dean, *The Nature of the Non-Western World* (New York, 1957).

5. N. J. G. Pounds, "Historical Geography of the Iron and Steel Industry of France," *Annals of the Association of American Geographers*, XLVII (1957), 3–14.

6. *Protokolle über die Vernehmungen der Sachverständigen durch die Eisen-Enquete-Kommission* (Berlin, 1878).

7. Aloys A. Michel, "The Canalization of the Moselle and West European Integration," *Geographical Review*, LII (1962), 475–91.

The Soviet Bloc, the Common Market, and France ZBIGNIEW K. BRZEZINSKI

"THE EAST WIND PREVAILS OVER THE WEST WIND," boasted Mao Tse-tung late in 1957. But the Chinese statesman was a few years behind the times. It is true that until the mid-fifties the West had little impact on the East, and it was the East that seemed to be shaping the historical destiny of the West. In Europe, the area beyond the Elbe river was hermetically sealed off from the rest of the continent, while Germany, France, and other west European countries lived in a state of almost continuous preoccupation with the fear of a new Soviet aggression. Gradually, the tables turned and the situation was reversed. The post-Stalin turmoil in the communist world, which today is reaching its climax in the Sino-Soviet rift, compels the communist leaders to seek more stable forms of political and economic international organization within their sphere of power. Just as important to this new relationship between the East and the West has been the emergence of the new Europe, for the time being restricted only to the western section but already a powerful economic force, capable of exerting with each passing day increased ideological and political appeal to the lands beyond the Elbe. Today, it is not western Europe that fears the East; it is in the Kremlin and in the communist capitals of eastern Europe that much thought is given to countervailing the growing appeal of European unity and to checking, somehow, the economic impact of the European Common Market.

The Treaty of Rome, establishing Euratom and the Common Market, was signed on March 25, 1957. It was not a sudden move nor was it signed merely on impulse. It came after many years of discussion and prolonged negotiations, and it was the climax of the efforts initiated by the Marshall Plan in the late 1940's. Yet, despite this lengthy prelude, the communist leaders seemed unable at first to perceive the Common Market's full implications, and their responses to this development have thus been characterized by a high degree of confusion and inconsistency.

THE SOVIET PERCEPTION OF THE PROBLEM

During the period since the signing of the Treaty of Rome, the Soviet analysis of developments in western Europe, of the Common Market, of the role of the United States, of the re-emergence of France, and of the new Franco-German relationship has undergone several radical revisions. In part, these revisions were necessitated by the rapid flow of events. It would be wrong to imply that flexibility of analysis is in itself proof of the inadequacy of the original analysis. But even a cursory examination of the Soviet views reveals that the Soviet policy-makers were struggling hard to perceive the implications of the new reality, which somehow did not fit their established and ideologically influenced categories, and that adjustments in their analyses were, more often than not, caused by belated recognition that their own original analysis had been wrong.

An examination of the major Soviet pronouncements and, even more important, of the discussions in the more serious and academic Soviet journals on foreign affairs suggests that the evolution and revision of Soviet thinking on this subject may be seen in terms of four successive major themes, each, of course, overlapping with the next. The latter qualification is important because it would be misleading to suggest that at any given point the Soviet mood was fixed and absolutely rigid; within a certain broad spectrum there was a continuous debate. The line of analysis, because of a general uncertainty as to how to assess this novel development in the "camp of imperialism," was more fluid than firm. Thus, broadly speaking, immediately prior to the Treaty of Rome and for a while afterward, Soviet spokesmen stressed the proposition that politically the Common Market was an American plot to subordinate Europe, while economically it was unimportant. In the late fifties, the emphasis shifted to the political threat represented by Germany or, as a variant, to the danger of a joint American-German hegemony; economically, the Common Market was seen in an ambivalent light— no longer simply dismissed as an insignificant irrelevance but not yet taken quite seriously. In the early sixties, the sense of uncertainty and ambivalence pervaded the political analysis, especially in defining the Soviet stand towards English participation in the Common Market, whereas economically the ambivalence gave way at best to a thinly veiled fear of the Common Market's impact on the communist world. Finally, from mid-1962, the political analyses began to lay primary emphasis on the Franco-German threat, while in the economic domain they welcomed the open manifestation of "imperialist contradictions." Throughout, however, the dominant views of any given period were contested by spokesmen either still holding to the antecedent views or already advancing positions which only subsequently became dominant. Furthermore, at every stage the classical Marxist proposition concerning monopolistic conflicts provided a standard frame of reference for the discussion.

In June, 1957, the authoritative Moscow Institute of World Economy and International Relations published its basic theses "On the Creation of the Common Market and Euratom,"[1] in which it dismissed categorically, as an illusory hope, the proposition advanced by some supporters of the treaty that eventually the treaty would make Europe independent of America. Soviet observers saw the treaty as expressing an inherent capitalist tendency toward domination "by one leading imperialist power over others"[2] and leading toward "American tutelage over France and the whole of Western Europe."[3] As a result, the west European countries would be "robbed" of any possibility of pursuing an independent economic policy.[4] The treaty was defined as "one of the most important links in the chain of Europe's economic and political subordination to the aggressive plans of U.S. monopoly capitalism."[5] However, that writer

141

warned (introducing a theme which subsequently was to become dominant) that the long-range beneficiary of the treaty would be West Germany.[6]

Remarkably, little attention was paid to the economic aspects of the undertaking. For example, a joint meeting of the editorial board of the important journal *International Affairs* and of the Department of Political Economy of the Academy of Social Sciences (the highest Party institution of learning) of the Central Committee of the Communist Party of the Soviet Union (CPSU) devoted to the subject "The Present Economic Situation in the Capitalist World" and held in April, 1958, barely deigned to mention the Common Market, and then only in passing, while concentrating attention on the more ideologically satisfactory matter of "the sharpening of contradictions" in western Europe.[7] The view tended to be that these contradictions were fundamentally insoluble and that the Common Market would founder on them.[6] However, there were a few isolated voices raised to the contrary. In a statement which explicitly acknowledged the existence of a controversy, one Soviet commentator argued that "it would be wrong to underestimate these efforts [i.e., the Common Market], to seek consolation in doubtful pronouncements that these plans cannot all the same be carried into life. Unfortunately, statements of this kind are found sometimes in the progressive press in the West and sometimes in sections of the Soviet press."[9] While this still seemed to be the minority point of view, it had been articulated even at the time of the signing of the Treaty of Rome.

During this period, Soviet political tactics accorded with the dominant generalizations. Little or no thought appears to have been given to the long-range effects of the Common Market on the communist countries in east Europe or on the Soviet Union. This negligence is to be explained in part by the disarray then prevailing in the Soviet bloc. The Hungarian revolution had taken place a mere half-year earlier; the new Gomulka regime in Poland was only in the process of defining its relations with Moscow; and the Soviet government was struggling to correct the Stalinist economic abuses committed against its satellites and, as a result, was being forced to extend credits and grants-in-aid to hitherto exploited allies. No wonder there seemed little time to reflect on the Common Market. Moscow satisfied itself with simple-minded denunciations and numerous appeals to the west European nations to defend their "sovereignty" against this new American imperialist encroachment.

Perhaps partly for tactical reasons, perhaps in part because of genuine fears, the Soviets also by 1958 had stepped up the theme of German domination in west Europe. Not surprisingly, warnings of this danger were most frequently addressed to France, in keeping with the broad thrust of Soviet propaganda directed at France since the initial steps taken by the West in the early fifties to promote West German rearmament. The Common Market was increasingly represented as a joint American-German conspiracy, designed particularly to subordinate France. Numerous articles appeared in Soviet journals, "proving" that West German monopolies were extending their sway over all of west Europe[10] and providing the underpinning for American political supremacy. French interests were seen as either sacrificed by disloyal French ruling classes or incapable of resisting this overwhelming onslaught. The irreconcilability of French and German national interests was the constant leitmotiv. Even after General de Gaulle had come to power, this view continued to dominate. Thus, although some Soviet commentators gradually came to concede that the French and German "bourgeoisies" had certain common interests, that outside the French Communist Party "there is no political group of any importance in France which demands an end to the policy of alliance with German militarism," and that there might even be some temporary benefits accruing to French big business from such a rapprochement, the argument always turned to the basic proposition that France was becoming West Germany's junior partner.[11] This was said to be inevitable, given the constellation of economic power. But here, too, occasional voices of dissent were heard. In mid-1959, the Soviet thinking public was exposed to the argument that De Gaulle was actually using Franco-German relations for purely expedient political reasons and that it would be premature to speak of West German economic domination. In fact, it was argued, France had been making important economic advances and "in brief, at the present moment French capital considers itself able to compete with German capital."[12] Perhaps not accidentally, this somewhat undoctrinaire view was advanced not by a Soviet but by a French Marxist writer, and it came at a time when Khrushchev was seriously contemplating the possibility of wooing De Gaulle directly (see below, Part III).

The earlier contemptuous dismissal of the economic aspects of the Common Market gradually gave way to greater, but rather ambivalent, interest. Internal economic difficulties were gleefully discussed, and much attention was devoted to the clash of interests between the European Economic Community (EEC) and the European Free Trade Association (EFTA). The conflict was held to validate the correctness of the original proposition that from an economic standpoint the enterprise was doomed to fail. Somewhat inconsistently, however, and certainly in conflict with the analysis made in 1957 by the Institute of World Economy and International Relations, by late 1959, the theme of European-American economic competition began to make its appearance. Thus, although France and Germany were still said to be in basic economic conflict, they were seen as already jointly challenging American hegemony, and Secretary Dillon's mission to Europe was described in December, 1959, as an effort to overcome west Europe's attempts "to weaken somewhat the course of American economic 'guidance.' "[13] Thus west European economic unity, said to be an impossibility, was portrayed as challenging American economic domination, was said to have been enhanced by American efforts to enforce that European unity!

Within a year, the original thesis of American domination was officially buried. In September, 1960, Yudin, a well-known Soviet writer on international affairs, declared that "in contemporary conditions the former U.S. approach to West European economic problems as only a means of reinforcing the NATO military bloc, is clearly outdated. The United States has lost control over the process of Western Europe's economic integration."[14] This was made authoritative a year later with Khrushchev's statement to the Twenty-second CPSU Congress which noted that the United States had lost its "absolute superiority" in the capitalist world economy and that this decline, shared also by England and France, was paralleled by the growing power of West Germany and Japan. However, to the Soviet leaders, the political implications seem to have been quite hazy. Khrushchev, for example, abandoning hope of interimperialist wars, still stressed intensifying contradictions and, at the same time, spoke of the decline of the United States, Britain, and France.

The crux of the uncertainty was the problem of English participation in the Common Market. Since the whole venture was described as an imperialist plot, first as purely American and then as increasingly taken over by the Franco-German bourgeoisie, it was difficult for the Soviet leaders to favor other nations' adherence to it. Furthermore, the Kremlin instinctively welcomed the conflict between EEC and EFTA, and the United Kingdom's entry in the Common Market would automatically spell the end of that particular "imperialist contradiction." (Furthermore, some communist states, for instance Poland, feared the economic consequences, particularly for their agricultural exports to the United Kingdom, of England's membership in EEC.) At the same time, however, the Soviet leaders were probably sincerely concerned lest the decline in relative American power be balanced by a consequent increase in German influence, or, possibly, a Franco-German constellation, thereby giving the Common Market a more anti-Soviet complexion. The Soviet leaders doubtless felt that German aspirations, given the division of Germany, were likely to be in more direct conflict with Soviet aspirations than the broader, and necessarily more defensive, American desire to forge an Atlantic Community, with its eastern limit on the Elbe.

Thus the Soviet leaders were torn by conflicting considerations. From an economic point of view, England's membership in the Common Market would be a further denial of the underlying premises of their ideological perspective; it would help to shape an even more powerful economic "capitalist" world; and it would be certain to have a further negative impact on Soviet and communist east European trade. More broadly still, it would intensify the historical appeal of European unity, a consideration which Moscow could not entirely neglect, given the revisionist mood among the

145

youth of east Europe and even Russia. By the middle of 1962, the Soviet leaders seem to have awakened to the realization that the Common Market was a reality, and, perhaps overcompensating for their past overoptimism about its "insoluble internal contradictions," they now began to speak of it as a powerful and dangerous instrument of imperialist aggression.[15] Any further expansion was therefore unwelcome. Yet, at the same time, there was something to be gained by English membership in the Common Market. Germany would be balanced; a more restrained, perhaps eventually even a pacifist, voice would be thus introduced (so the Soviets reasoned) into its political councils, and the entire political structure would become more complex.[16] This seemed desirable. To Moscow, as it began to perceive belatedly the emergence of the Franco-German constellation,[17] England now looked like a good counterweight.[18]

This political ambivalence about England was matched by a growing and open concern over the economic implications of the Common Market, and the two together made for a very uncertain general line. In May, 1962, Khrushchev delivered a major attack on the Common Market and urged that in its stead an international conference be convened to produce a world-wide trade organization of which the communist bloc would also be a part.[19] His speech left little doubt that the Common Market was now being taken seriously and was being interpreted not only as a direct threat to the communist world but also as an effective mechanism for establishing closer bonds between the Western world and the developing nations. New theses of the Institute of World Economy and International Relations, published shortly afterward, while still speaking about the "knot of imperialist contradictions," and while now also noting the French and German claims to leadership in Europe, grudgingly acknowledged that the Common Market could "provide an impetus to increasing the volume of production and of domestic and foreign trade." This was coupled with a strong plea for the most-favored-nation principle, hailed "as a universal and generally recognized principle of international affairs."[20] These proposals were clearly not being made from a position of economic strength.

Soviet optimism was given a new lease on life by General de Gaulle's press conference of January 14, 1963. Triumphantly proclaiming that "this confirms what Marxists have said all along: underneath the thin crust of 'Atlantic Unity' there boils the hot lava of imperialist contradictions,"[21] the Soviets for the time being laid aside their fears of Franco-German imperialism and saw in the event renewed proof of the West's inevitable decline. The whole Western alliance was represented as being at stake, and, while the Soviet reporting of the event on the whole took a sympathetic tone toward Britain's plight, the dominant note was clearly one of jubilation. But more somber voices were also heard, and it did not take long for Moscow to perceive that fundamentally not much had been really changed, that the economic threat still persisted, and that in some ways the political picture had perhaps now become more ominous, if clearer, than before. V. Nekrasov, writing in *Izvestia*, warned his readers that the exclusion of Britain facilitated the transformation of the Common Market into a political-military bloc (the theme of contradictions being quietly ignored), and by the middle of the year Moscow was addressing urgent pleas to Paris not to further the nuclear rearmament of West Germany, and unashamedly appealing to the pride of the French (who only a short time ago were being portrayed as German vassals): "It will be no exaggeration to say that if the Soviet Union and France, the two greatest powers of the European continent, were to act in concert on the basic issues on which the future of Europe depends, then no forces could rise up and attempt to redraw the map of Europe."[22] Contempt thus gave way to flattery, and the change was caused both by the impact on the East of the Common Market and by the reappearance of a French foreign policy.[23]

The foregoing discussion suggests that the Soviet perception of the Common Market was impeded by: (1) an ideological rigidity, with its strong emphasis on "inherent" economic contradictions in capitalism; (2) an assumption that old national hatreds in Europe would endure, particularly the Franco-German hatred; (3) a fixation on the American position in Europe and the resulting tendency to judge everything in terms of it; (4) an overestimation of the

147

importance of the failure of The European Defense Community (EDC) and hence also the belief that EEC would fail; and finally, (5) a general ignorance of developments in the West, an ignorance caused by lack of personal contacts and by a lack of empathy with the dominant trends of thought in the West—both being the outcome of many years of isolation.*

THE IMPACT OF THE COMMON MARKET

The development of the Common Market created several basic problems for the Soviet and east European communist leaders. The first was in the realm of ideology, which hardly requires much elaboration for a reader familiar with even the rudiments of Marxist-Leninist doctrines. The Common Market defied communist predictions and assumptions, and by 1962 a thorough re-examination of some fundamental assumptions about internal "imperialist contradictions" and about the alleged negative internal economic consequences of the Common Market, especially in so far as the working class was concerned, was very much in order.

This was undertaken by a special conference of Marxists from twenty-three countries held in Moscow in late August, 1962, and devoted exclusively to "the problems of contemporary capitalism." The focus of the conference was the Common Market, but it was not contemporary capitalism that was dissected and discussed at the conference table; it was the communist perspective that was debated and eventually revised. On the eve of the conference, *Pravda* published an appeal to the participants to expose the Common Market as a "criminal plot," and it may be presumed that the Soviet delegates went to it with a position generally reflecting the then existing attitude of the Soviet government. The conference, however, prompted a very vigorous debate in which the intellectual leadership was quickly assumed by non-Soviet Marxists, primarily the Italians, supported by the Poles and some other east Europeans. The Soviets were reported to have received solid backing from the French.[24] The argument which the Italians advanced was simply a statement of fact; namely, that the working class in Europe was

---

* Professor Robert Byrnes suggested these helpful generalizations.

actually also benefiting from the Common Market and that the Common Market had to be accepted as a fact of life. The closing remarks of the Soviet spokesman, A. A. Arzumanian, the director of the Institute of World Economy and International Relations, were, in effect, an admission that the previous ideological perspective had proven itself inadequate, and an exhortation to all Marxists to work together in order to define more accurately the nature of this novel development and the thrust of its further evolution.[25]

The persistence of ideological ambiguities and perplexities was brought to light shortly afterward at the December Leipzig meeting of the World Federation of Trade Unions. As in Moscow, the debate over the Common Market again pitted the Italian communist spokesmen ("the realists") against the French, supported by the Soviets ("the doctrinarians"). The arguments covered the same ground as in the previous conference, but it is noteworthy that the Italians obtained even somewhat more overt support from the Poles, the Yugoslavs, and the Czechs. For the latter three, the Common Market raised not only ideological problems but very immediate economic dilemmas, and this contributed to their inclination toward the "realist" position. Again, the issue was not resolved, but the continuing debate, as well as the search for some common formula, has in the meantime contributed to the steady relativization of the Soviet position, thereby weakening the hold of some hitherto semi-sacred absolutes. In that way, the Common Market has had a significant impact on the communist ideological world perspective.[26]

This, however, did not cause any decrease in anti–Common Market propaganda. In fact, precisely because the Common Market is gradually being accepted as a permanent factor of our times, its long-range danger to the homogeneity of the communist world is seen as all the greater. Communist leaders increasingly perceive that the European idea, resting on this "economic base" (to use their own category), is gaining in potency, particularly in the most western areas of the Soviet sphere, and might eventually infect the U.S.S.R. itself. Thus, admitting quite explicitly that the European idea has a great deal of appeal, even to the working classes, which are said to applaud the concept of a "United States of Europe," one Polish communist writer, obviously concerned over the impact of the idea on Poland, found himself arguing the proposition that European economic community "is not a unity and will not be one, even when it becomes the form in fact."[27] Other communist propagandists took on the recently published *European History*, sponsored by the Council of Europe, and vehemently rejected its thesis of basic harmony in European history, thereby, in effect, pleading the cause of nationalism.[28] Many other examples could be cited, all testifying to growing concern lest the European idea become the dominant vision of the future in the communist sphere itself.

If a sense of weakness and concern was discernible in the realm of ideology, it was even more warranted and apparent in the case of the economic impact. The simple fact of the matter was that trade with western Europe was more important to the communist states than to western Europe, and the development of the Common Market, with its internal tariff arrangements and new internal trade patterns, was thus a formidable threat. The table that follows was computed by comparing the trade of a given east European country

TABLE 7

COMPARATIVE IMPORTANCE OF TRADE IN EEC NATIONS
AND EAST EUROPEAN COMMUNIST COUNTRIES,
IN 1961, IN APPROXIMATE RATIOS [29]

	Belgium and Luxembourg	Netherlands	West Germany	France	Italy
Bulgaria	1:6.0	1:8.8	1:20.3	1:11.3	1:7.8
Czechoslovakia	1:2.0	1:2.3	1:5.9	1:3.2	1:2.3
German Democratic Republic	1:1.8	1:2.2	1:7.0	1:3.0	1:2.0
Hungary	1:4.0	1:4.5	1:11.9	1:6.9	1:4.6
Poland	1:2.6	1:3.0	1:7.5	1:4.3	1:3.0
Rumania	1:5.0	1:4.5	1:15.0	1:8.4	1:5.9
U.S.S.R.	1:0.7	1:0.9	1:1.9	1:1.2	1:0.9

Total ratio of CEMA to EEC: 1:2.3

with a member nation of the Common Market to the total world trade of each country, thereby establishing the relative importance of that trade to the communist and the west European nations respectively. It yields some rather striking results.

The above calculations show that with the partial exception of the Soviet Union the trade relationship was far more significant to the communist states than to the members of the Common Market (for example, in the case of Bulgaria, its trade with Belgium-Luxembourg involved a percentage of its entire trade six times higher than the corresponding proportion of Belgium-Luxembourg's trade with Bulgaria, relative to Belgium-Luxembourg's total world trade). This simple formula, of course, does not take into account the nature of the goods exchanged, the degree of diversification in exports, the availability of other markets, and so on; but it may suffice as a general indicator. And while, in the case of some of these communist states, trade with the Common Market did not represent a very significant portion of their total trade, by and large it did represent a major part of their total trade with the "capitalist" world, and it was a prime source of hard currency.

Because of these considerations, communist leaders feared the consequences of lowering customs in the turnover between the Common Market countries, combined with the introduction of uniform customs duties in respect to non-member nations. They were also concerned lest the efforts to establish a common agricultural policy, with self-sufficiency as the object, affect adversely the exports of some of the east European countries. Finally, they were uneasy lest the joint efforts of the Common Market to establish a general commercial policy regarding non-members give the Economic Community a new lever in dealings with the East. This was stated quite frankly: "A common commercial policy of the Common Market countries creates the possibility of a simultaneous stopping of imports or exports by all six countries. Let us just recall the embargo from the recent period of the cold war to realize in full the danger contained in this intention of the Common Market countries."[30]

Thundering against the Common Market and describing it as a political-economic plot constituted the external reaction to its economic impact. The internal consequence was the further acceleration of efforts to develop the Council for Economic Mutual Assistance (CEMA), a long-dormant Stalinist institution revitalized in the mid-fifties in order to compensate for the decline in direct Soviet political control,[31] and now urgently activated in response to the challenge of the Common Market. From 1960 on, this effort has been pursued in earnest. The economic specialization of member nations has been introduced into several branches of Soviet heavy industry; preliminary steps have been taken to establish broad guidelines (over a twenty-year period) for national economic planning; and, after a long delay, the first multilateral economic institutions of the bloc have begun to make their appearance. The operations of CEMA were also regularized and institutionalized (hitherto it had been largely an *ad hoc* body), and in mid-1961 a formal charter was promulgated, outlining in some detail its scope and *modus operandi*. In October, 1963, the CEMA agreement was signed, providing for a common bank for clearing purposes based on a gold ruble (a scheme obviously based on earlier western European experience). Energetic efforts were also being made to create the necessary statistical basis for effective common planning (a matter of particular importance, given the absence of the market mechanism), in addition to undertaking several multilateral economic projects (common pipelines, rail stock, communication cables, and so on).[32]

That these efforts were dictated both by the internal needs of the bloc and by the challenge from the outside was almost explicitly admitted. In mid-1962, after the Moscow conference of First Secretaries of the Central Committees of the Communist and Workers' Parties and heads of governments of CEMA members, Khrushchev published a major statement devoted to the problem of economic co-ordination of the Soviet bloc. He acknowledged that the Common Market reflected "the objective tendency toward even greater internationalization of economic life" and conceded that it provided "tremendous advantages for the imperialist monopolies." In his plea for more international division of labor and co-operation within CEMA, Khrushchev somewhat defensively acknowledged that the Common Market was ahead in these respects, and in a curious reversal of Marxist priorities he explained that the Soviet bloc already had forged its poltical unity but must now achieve the same result in economics. His speech was noteworthy for its admissions of failure in capital circulation, in stimulating a higher volume of trade within CEMA, and in developing multilateral planning in both trade and production.[33]

The economic impact of the Common Market had another, and curious, internal consequence for the communist world. Khrushchev alluded to it in his statement just cited when he vaguely observed that "in our time the full utilization of the economic laws of socialism means learning to study how to throw light on their operation, to consider them not only in a national framework but also on the international scale." A more explicit reference was made in a special editorial of the Party's ideological organ, *Kommunist*, published on the occasion of the 1962 Moscow conference, which attacked efforts to build socialism in isolation on the basis of autarky, labeling this as nationalism, "which in our contemporary conditions represents much the greatest danger to the unity and solidarity of the socialist commonwealth."[34] That these warnings were not meant only for faraway China (in any case, a non-member of CEMA) was made plain in an article which appeared in *Mirovaia Ekonomika i Mezhdunarodnye Otnosheniia* in the fall of 1962. Its author quite sharply attacked again the notion of economic autarky, revealing this time that the criticism was directed at those who allege that "the socialist division of labor" assigns to some countries an agrarian economy, and to others an industrial role, thereby confirming reports circulating in the West that the Rumanian leadership was objecting to some aspects of this "division," since they seemed directed at Rumanian industrial development. Pleading for a rational development of specialization, based on the criterion of efficiency, the Soviet author stressed that it would be compatible with the specific interests of individual countries and he pinned the label "nationalism" on its opponents.[35]

That economically "rational" specialization might, however, be incompatible with specific national interests was a strong probability

153

in the Soviet bloc, given the wide disparities in levels of industrial development and proficiency. Applied strictly, it was bound to favor the more industrially developed nations, i.e., the U.S.S.R., the German Democratic Republic, and Czechoslovakia. As a result, it was opposed by the less developed states, and in 1962-63 especially by Rumania, which saw favorable opportunities for its own industrial development. A Rumanian spokesman thus explicitly rejected the primacy of the principle of efficiency: "Just as on the internal scene absolutism in criterion of efficiency cannot be countenanced, in the field of specialization and co-operation between the socialist countries, economic efficiency and profitability cannot be the one and only criterion with which to measure the new economic steps."[36] The Rumanian writer then neatly turned the tables on the Soviets by suggesting that a division of labor which perpetuates agrarian and industrial economies is essentially a "bourgeois" and an "imperialist" theory for which there is no place in the "socialist camp." Finally, contrary to "friendly" warnings from Soviet writers against "a mechanical copying" of the Soviet stress on industrial development,[37] the Rumanian devoted a great deal of attention to proving that under the conditions of "socialism" the rapid industrial development of backward countries was especially facilitated and that a relatively backward country such as Rumania would therefore develop her industrial section more rapidly than Czechoslovakia or East Germany.[38] His argument was punctuated by categorical assertions such as, "Building Communism on a worldwide scale is incompatible with the notion of dividing countries into industrial states and agrarian states, into developed countries and underdeveloped countries," and "Socialist industrialization is for our country a major preoccupation—it is an objective necessity, the successful realization of which will determine the victory of socialism and communism."[39]

Refuting the issue raised by the Rumanians was made more difficult by two factors: (1) the development of the Common Market which, on the one hand, involved the rapid industrial development of a relatively backward country such as Italy (thereby creating an embarrassing example) and, on the other, could present the Rumanians with tempting trade arrangements (the French, for example, have already shown an interest in developing the Rumanian oil industry); and (2) the internal complications within the communist world. The Chinese, in their attacks on Moscow, have pointedly raised the matter of discriminatory economic development, and this item the Rumanians prominently republished in their own press. As a result, both the Soviet and the east European reactions have been marked by an effort to find some intermediate solution, without either abandoning the long-range goal of economically rational division of labor or entirely ignoring the Rumanian aspirations. The public discussion, however, has shown that the issue is not only complex but that divergent economic and political interests are involved.[40] Here again, the relative ability of the Common Market to solve similar problems was bound to intrude in the communist discussions.

Indeed, one may justifiably suspect that the Chinese resentment of the Soviet failure to help Chinese economic development adequately was fed by the sight of extensive and effective American aid to Europe. The spectacular European recovery contrasted sharply with continued Chinese failures and with disinterested Soviet passivity and contributed to internal communist dissension.

The economic and the ideological impact of the Common Market thus challenged the basic communist proposition that Communists have a key to the future. Given the complications in CEMA, it was even uncertain whether they could control their own future. A major tenet of their doctrine, namely, that there are inherent unresolvable contradictions within "imperialism," was now subject to doubt; and Khrushchev finally acknowledged this when, in pleading for more trade (from a position, as noted, of relative economic weakness), he conceded that "the question arises of the possibility of economic co-operation and peaceful economic competition not only between individual states with different social systems but also between their economic federations."[41] However, with the failure of the Soviets to resolve the Berlin issue in their favor, and with the gradual re-emergence of France as an independent European force, the Soviet leadership had also to give more and more thought to the longer-range political challenge of an increasingly powerful and self-assertive western Europe.

The political challenge was personalized by De Gaulle and expressed through the assertively independent French policy for Europe. The short-range aspect of this policy pertained to the more immediate problem of the organization and distribution of power in the West; the longer-range aspect, to the definition of a new relationship with the East. By 1963, the outlines of the former were clear; the shape of the latter, although still vague, was no longer undefinable.

De Gaulle's Western policy can be very briefly summarized.[42] It rested on his twin confidence in the durability of west Europe's new economic structure and in the capacity of the United States to deter any Soviet military action against western Europe. If the basic European motive of the late forties can be said to have been fear of Soviet aggression, in the early sixties it tended to be self-confidence. Taking that confidence as his point of departure, De Gaulle was able to press steadily for diminution of American political influence on the Continent, hoping to replace it by a Franco-German concord. Given the limits imposed on German rearmament and, more important, the moral and political inhibitions which still conditioned the German outlook, it was reasonable to assume that the political (and perhaps also military) leadership in that relationship would inevitably be exercised by France. To assure that end, and also to increase Europe's influence on American military policy (at least to the point of achieving the capacity to involve America even in spite of America's desires), De Gaulle undertook to transform France into a nuclear power. The long-range importance of nuclear development, in his view, more than compensated for the temporary isolation and even unpopularity of France. These considerations were the logical outgrowth of his rejection of the Anglo-Saxon conception of the Atlantic Community, in which he saw the political and military power controlled almost entirely from Washington and London. A tightly integrated western Europe subject to such "external" control would be a Europe "without soul, without backbone, and without roots," subject "to one or the other of the two foreign hegemonies." [43]

Furthermore, in his view, such a Europe would become a pliant tool of the two superpowers, the United States and the U.S.S.R., which, in fact, had no incompatible interests in Europe at the time. Moscow, it would seem, no longer expected to be able to swallow up (in the near future, at least) the rest of Europe, and was content to remain on the Elbe, busy consolidating its rear. America, despite the phraseology of her leaders, accepted that division and would certainly make no effort to re-establish European unity. This De Gaulle has stated quite openly: "The United States, which since Yalta and Potsdam has had nothing to demand from the Soviets, now sees prospects of understanding opening before it. The result is the separate negotiations between the Anglo-Saxons and the Soviets, which, starting from the restricted nuclear test agreement, appear about to be extended to other questions, notably European questions, and so far in the absence of Europeans. This obviously runs counter to the views of France." Having charged America with complicity in the division of Europe, De Gaulle then asserted that the day would come when "a complete change in the relations between East and West in Europe" would become possible and that "when this day comes, and I have said this before, France expects to make constructive proposals concerning the peace, equilibrium, and destiny of Europe." [44]

De Gaulle has given several hints what these "constructive proposals" might be: in brief, they involve the absorption of east Europe and Russia into a larger European community based on common cultural and historical heritage and defined by geography. In March, 1959, the French leader launched the slogan of "Europe to the Urals," linking it to an eloquent plea for a common European enterprise:

> We, who live between the Atlantic and the Urals, we, who are Europe, possessing with Europe's daughter, America, the principal sources and resources of civilization . . . why do we not pool a percentage of our raw

materials, our manufactured goods, our food products, some of our scientists, technologists, economists, some of our trucks, ships, and aircraft in order to vanquish misery, develop the resources, and the trust in work, of less developed peoples? Let us do this not that they should be the pawns of our policies, but to improve the chances of life and peace. How much more worthwhile that would be than the territorial demands, ideological claims, imperialist ambitions which are leading the world to its death! [45]

Since then, De Gaulle has frequently alluded to this conception, and it is clear that he sees its realization as culminating a lengthy process of transformation within the communist states, perhaps accelerated by the reactive effect of the Sino-Soviet conflict and the growing attraction of Europe and the Common Market.[46] Accordingly, De Gaulle has cultivated China, hoping that Russia's new encirclement might even make her anxious to become part of Europe.

To prepare the groundwork for the maturation of this process, De Gaulle, in spite of his close ties with Germany (which he sees as the backbone for independent European action), has been determined to undermine gradually the traditional fear of the east Europeans of a renewed German *Drang nach Osten*. Thus he has gone further than Washington in indicating his acceptance of the present Polish-German frontier on the Oder and Neisse rivers as permanent,[47] an acknowledgment which constitutes the *sine qua non* for any drawing of Poland back into the European orbit. And Poland, given her geographic location and present special links with Russia, would be the vital link in any eventual return of Russia to a European orientation.[48]

There is a strong element of French *sacro egoismo* and deception in the General's preoccupation with east Europe. In his mind, to the extent that the idea of Europe is synonymous with French leadership, it follows that the two best alternatives for France are either (1) a Europe divided on the Elbe, in which a divided Germany depends on France for its eventual reunification, or (2) a united Europe including not only a seventy-million-strong Germany but also east Europe (and even Russia), which with France would more than balance German might. That is why Paris could now hardly welcome a German reunification that would leave east Europe in the hands of hostile—and perhaps even fearful—Russians. And that is why Paris welcomes and yet abuses the present American policy toward Germany which implicitly accepts the division on the Elbe while explicitly preaching reunification but with the eastern frontiers of Germany undefined (thus giving the Poles no alternative but to support Moscow and Pankow wholeheartedly). For the time being, this policy suits Paris well, for it makes it possible to gain German support simply by adopting a more militant stand on such issues as Berlin. Indeed, at the moment, German *immobilisme* on the subject of frontiers or the Hallstein doctrine and American passivity about the division of Europe are in keeping with De Gaulle's timetable: it being too early to move in the East, it is important to forge Franco-German political unity in the West at the expense of "passive" America. Joint American-German efforts now, involving the recognition of the Oder-Neisse line and attempts at a political-economic penetration of eastern Europe, would find France unprepared and unable to exercise her leadership. In time, Germany will realize the futility of the American approach,[49] and the moment will be ripe to seek actively, under French leadership, a "Europe to the Urals." (Could the Soviet realm beyond the Urals be an inducement for the Chinese?)

The Soviet reaction to the unfolding of De Gaulle's design has been guarded, but signs of mounting concern have been multiplying. Initially, the Soviets seemed to welcome France's restiveness simply because it represented a new complication for the arch rival, the United States.[50] The Soviet leaders repeatedly stressed their desire to see France play a greater and more independent (i.e., anti-American) role in international affairs,[51] and they presumably hoped that De Gaulle's leadership would provide a further impetus in that direction. *Pravda*, for instance, made a point of recalling that the Soviet Union, quite unlike the United States, had given the strongest backing to De Gaulle's wartime Committee of National Liberation; [52] and Khrushchev, both before and after his March, 1960, visit to Paris, stressed his respect for the General and the "friendly" relations established with him.[53] Parallel efforts were made to invigorate Franco-Soviet trade, which had grown steadily in the late fifties, and which in 1958 for the first time passed the level achieved in 1913.[54] The growth of France was clearly linked in the Soviet mind with the decline of American power in Europe.

Although for a time hopeful that the resurgence of France under De Gaulle might weaken the West, the Soviets from the start were quite sensitive to any signs of French interest in east Europe. Thus, after Adenauer's visit to Paris in the early fall of 1958, Khrushchev in a special "interview" singled out for criticism a phrase in the De Gaulle-Adenauer communiqué about eventual inclusion of "the maximum possible number of European states" in a European federation. To Khrushchev, this meant that De Gaulle and Adenauer "must have lost all sense of reality to count seriously on success in any venture in Eastern Europe." [55] This point he reiterated two days later in an interview with a German journalist.[56]

These fears mounted as the Franco-German alliance took shape. Denunciatory tones quickly became dominant, and it was clear that by 1960 the Soviet leadership had reappraised the French role and was beginning to see in it a long-range political danger. France was represented not only as seeking the domination of western Europe,[57] but also as encouraging the proliferation of nuclear weapons,[58] and as being led by an Olympian figure who had lost all sense of reality.[59] By 1962, France was frequently represented as the chief brake on relaxation of international tensions.[60] De Gaulle's trip to Germany was officially attacked as part of a plot to establish a "Europe to the Urals" (this phrase was quoted), which would involve the liquidation of the communist regimes in east Europe by means of joint Franco-German co-operation and include also the sharing of nuclear weapons.[61] The denunciations reached their peak in 1963 after France's refusal to sign the test-ban agreement.

Since De Gaulle's plans appear vague even to his own followers, they probably also appear vague to the Soviets. Yet the very vagueness of his design—with its strong overtones of assertiveness towards Russia and east Europe—might seem to the Soviets more dangerous than the known, and basically static, Anglo-American "interest" in the areas east of the Elbe. As a result, the Soviet attitude toward the American position in Europe became more ambivalent. Thus, from a political point of view, the possibility of a Franco-German challenge based on continental Europe represented a greater threat than the American-sponsored Atlantic Community. Yet from an economic and even more from a military point of view, it was certainly America and NATO that posed by far the greater threat. How to reconcile these alternatives became increasingly the dominant Soviet dilemma, and by 1963 the Soviets were somewhat less willing than, for instance, the Chinese to view with equanimity the prospect of American political exclusion from the continent.[62] Instead, the Soviets were more and more inclined to try to maneuver the United States into the position of joint sponsorship of the division of Europe, in the hope of stabilizing the present partition and, perhaps, eventually of creating new political opportunities for Soviet diplomacy.

In this regard, the confrontation in Cuba in late 1962 was a particularly important watershed. It convinced the Soviets that for the time being their means were inadequate to their ends, and that the Soviet policy of pressing, both politically and militarily, for a breakthrough in Europe by means of the squeeze on Berlin was doomed to fail, and, in fact, was already counterproductive. America would not yield, and the effect of the pressure was to strengthen the "aggressive" forces in France and Germany. But by striving for a Soviet-American rapprochement, based on acceptance by Washington of the division of Europe, the Franco-German challenge might be converted into a bitter and destructive internal Western feud, with even the ultimate possibility of a new Rapallo. Apparently resigned for the time being to French and German hostility, Moscow decided to make certain that the Franco-German alignment was denied American political and military backing. Thus, Moscow has vigorously opposed the American scheme for establishing a European Multilateral Nuclear Force (MLF), which would help to consolidate American-European political and military ties. However, since failure to set up MLF would further increase the attractiveness to Bonn of General de Gaulle's policies, with the end result possibly being even an independent German nuclear force, or at least a joint Franco-German force serving the political ambitions of Paris and Bonn (ambitions inherently less compatible with the Soviet desire to maintain her control over the captive areas of Europe than is the case with the analogous American goals), the Soviet opposition to MLF thus played into the hands of Paris. The inability to resolve this dilemma contributed to Soviet ambivalence and reflected the growing complexity of the Soviet position in Europe.

Jointly, Russia and America could maintain the division of Europe, but there would be no guarantee that at some moment Russia might not choose to exploit European frustrations against America, Russia's real global competitor. Russo-American sponsorship of the division of Europe would hence be inherently unstable and dangerous to America. A European-Russian collaboration against America could only arise as a consequence of European resentment of American leadership and out of a sense of American betrayal of European interests. Accordingly, it would have to be proceded by an American-Soviet *détente,* based on joint acceptance of the status quo in Europe, a goal which the Soviet Union is now seeking. Without this preliminary, a European-Russian collaboration appears most unlikely, given the Soviet desire to perpetuate her hegemony over half of Europe, and the increasingly overt west European determination to challenge that hegemony. An American-European collaboration designed to reunite Europe and to reintegrate Russia in the Western civilization, a process now abetted by the Sino-Soviet schism, appears to be the most potent and the most enduring combination, one that reflects the long-range interests of both America and Europe.

More than ever, Russia is now becoming susceptible to the attraction of Europe. In the past, the Russian attitude toward Europe had fluctuated. On the one hand, there was arrogant talk of Moscow being the Third Rome, then of its being the source of a new and universal ideology. On the other hand, there was a deep-seated sense of inferiority to the West and a desire to imitate it. The

Russian Communists combined the sense of superiority with a drive to erase the inferiority (through imitation, i.e., industrialization). By narrowing the technical, economic, and cultural gap between Europe and Russia, the Soviet leaders have created for the first time the possibility of a relationship that is equal and honorable to both. Meanwhile, the Sino-Soviet schism marred the universalist aspect of the ideology, while Soviet control of eastern Europe not only has diminished Russian fears of the West but also has created a transmission belt for Western values. Without knowing it, the Soviet leaders have performed the historical function of preparing the ground for a larger Europe, but—alas for them— not a communist one.

The challenge of France is the first sign that Europe is now looking ahead, is no longer fearful for her survival but is seeking the fulfillment of her centuries-long destiny. This reawakening necessarily has involved a realignment of power in the West, with consequent tensions in the Western alliance. But France's real challenge points eastward. In ideology, the idea of European unity, with the Common Market as the initial symbol, is proving itself a more captivating and a more accurate image of the future than the Marxist-Leninist hopes for continued inter-European conflicts. In its economy, western Europe has shown a far more impressive development of trade, pooling of common resources, and general improvement of the standard of living than have the communist countries. In politics, the public debates and disagreements among Western powers have still been far less intense and bitter than the parallel conflicts and reciprocal excommunications among the communist states, particularly those of Russia and China. All this gives the West an advantageous platform from which to invite the East to abandon its futile and old-fashioned ideological positions and to join in an undertaking that is also in its interest.

This could be done jointly by America and western Europe in a variety of ways, ranging from initial long-term bilateral trade arrangements to an eventual, multilateral economic-development plan based on the principle of European unity. Step by step, insistently,

163

the east European states should be encouraged to become associated, remotely and indirectly at first, and then more and more closely and directly, with the Common Market. West Europe could also take the initiative in opening its frontiers to the youth of the East—and leave it to the communist regimes, if they wish, to prevent their young people from sharing in growing European unity. It is doubtful that such pressure, so clearly in the interest of the peoples concerned, could long be resisted, even by their communist governments. To be sure, resist they will; and the present efforts to develop rapidly the institutions and operations of CEMA reflect the leaders' realization that without a strong economic framework the Soviet bloc will be unable to match the West and to contain the forces of national self-assertion within. Their efforts should not be underrated, but for the time being the conception of a united Europe is still ideologically more appealing and economically more promising. Unless the Soviet Union succeeds in enlisting America's support on behalf of the status quo, or unless western Europe fails to exploit its present opportunity and just passively observes the reconsolidation of the Soviet bloc, Europe is not likely to remain long "without soul, without backbone, and without roots."

1. *Kommunist*, June, 1957, pp. 88–102.

2. D. Mel'nikov, "A Threat to European Security," *International Affairs*, March, 1957, pp. 46–65.

3. I. Chelnokov, "The European Coal and Steel Community," *ibid.*, February, 1957, pp. 94–104.

4. Mel'nikov, *op. cit.*

5. Chelnokov, *op. cit.*

6. See also V. Liubimova, "The Problems of France's Participation in the 'Common Market,'" *Mirovaia Ekonomika i Mezhdunarodnye Otnosheniia*, No. 3, 1957, who argued that the chief beneficiary would be West Germany, acting as the United States agent.

7. *International Affairs*, May, 1958, pp. 76–102.

8. Quite typical is V. Knyazhinsky, "United Europe: A Weapon of Imperialist Policy," *ibid.*, June, 1957, pp. 51–58.

9. Mel'nikov, *op. cit.*

10. E.g., A. Galkin, "Expansion of the West German Monopolies in Europe," *International Affairs*, May, 1958, pp. 48–55.

11. See, for example, M. Lvov and A. Mishin, "France and West Germany," *International Affairs*, April, 1959, pp. 21–29.

12. Pierre Courtade, "The Paris-Bonn Axis and the Future of Europe," *International Affairs*, July, 1959, pp. 18–24.

13. *Pravda*, December 12, 1959. See also A. Galkin, "The Knot of Contradictions in Western Europe," *International Affairs*, August, 1959, pp. 43–49.

14. Y. Yudin, "What Is Behind the 'Four Wise Men's' Plan," *International Affairs*, September, 1960, pp. 47–53.

15. Quite characteristic is the commentary by V. Cherpakov, "The Common Market—An Instrument for the Intensification of Monopolistic Oppression and Aggression," *Kommunist*, May, 1962, pp. 22–35.

16. E.g., I. Lemin, "European Integration: Some Results and Perspectives," *Mirovaia Ekonomika i Mezhdunarodnye Otnosheniia*, April, 1962, pp. 21–36.

17. Some Soviet observers went as far as to negate their previous warnings about "German hegemony" and talked about "French hegemony in western Europe." For example, see Lemin, *ibid.*, Part II, May, 1962, pp. 42–55; and Cherpakov, *op. cit.*

18. For a good example of such conflicting motivations, see Viktor Mayevsky's correspondence from England in *Pravda*, August 29, 1962.

19. Although proposals of this sort had been advanced before, Khrushchev's statement displayed a degree of urgency and hostility not characteristic of earlier, and more self-assured, declarations. Cf., e.g., E. Menzhinsky and Y. Sergeev, "Peaceful Coexistence and Perspectives for the Development of European Economic Ties," *Mirovaia Ekonomika i Mezhdunarodnye Otnosheniia*, February, 1960, pp. 17–29.

20. *Pravda*, August 26, 1962. For a more ideological, and also oversimplified restatement of these themes, see V. Gantman, "Imperialist Integration and International Relations," *Kommunist*, November, 1962, pp. 96–107. For their further elaboration, with the help of east and west European Marxists, see the proceedings of the Moscow conference on contemporary capitalism, Summer, 1962, published in *Mirovaia Ekonomika i Mezhdunarodnye Otnosheniia*, November and December, 1962, pp. 54–71 and 59–79, respectively. These discussions cast a particularly interesting light on the role of non-Russian Marxists in enlightening their Russian friends about the state of affairs in Europe.

21. *New Times* (Moscow), January 30, 1963.

22. Soviet note to France of May 17, 1963, *Pravda*, May 20, 1963 (italics added).

23. The foregoing discussion of the Soviet perception of the problem benefited much from M. Shulman's article, "The Communist States and Western Integration," *International Organization*, Summer, 1963, pp. 649–63, although our interpretations of the various stages of Soviet reaction differ somewhat. I am grateful to Mr. Shulman for letting me see an advance copy of his article.

24. *Times* (London), September 6, 1962.

25. See *Mirovaia Ekonomika i Mezhdunarodnye Otnosheniia*, Nos. 11 and 12, 1962; also the *New York Times*, September 4, 1962. For Arzumanian's general views, see his *Krizis Mirovogo Kapitalizma na Sovremennom Etape*, Moscow, 1962.

26. This subject has been ably and more fully treated by Shulman in the article cited above (note 23).

27. *Zycie Warszawy*, September 9, 1963.

28. L. Krasucki, "The Dreamland of Historical Integration," *Trybuna Ludu*, August 30, 1963.

29. Sources: For east European trade, *Economic Bulletin for Europe* (United Nations), XIV, No. 1 (September, 1962), 47 (Table 19), 84–85 (Table A). For western European trade, *Direction of International Trade* ("Statistical Papers Series T," Vol. XIII, No. 1 [United Nations, International Monetary Fund, International Bank for Reconstruction and Development, January, 1963]).

30. W. Wirski, "Poland's Commerce with the Countries of the Common Market," *Zycie Gospodarcze*, August 11–18, 1963. The paragraph preceding the citation is based on Wirski. In February, 1963, the Common Market did begin to put into effect common regulations concerning some agricultural imports from the East (See *East Europe*, October, 1963, p. 34).

Presumably, because of this fear, some communist spokesmen have shown interest in a trial balloon, launched in the late summer of 1963 by Austrian Foreign Minister Kreisky, proposing an EFTA–CEMA trade agreement. (E.g., *Rynki Zagraniczne*, September 14, 1963.) In September, 1963, EEC made its first joint tariff move with respect to the U.S.S.R., demanding Soviet acceptance of the EEC tariff while offering the benefits of the lower internal EEC tariff to four Soviet export items (*Le Monde* [weekly ed.], October 17–23, 1963).

31. See my *The Soviet Bloc—Unity and Conflict* (Cambridge, 1960), esp. pp. 170–72.

32. For a discussion of these developments, titled quite revealingly, see M. Senin, "International Socialist Division of Labor and Competition between Two Systems," *Mirovaia Ekonomika i Mezhdunarodnye Otnosheniia*, No. 8, 1962.

33. *Kommunist*, August, 1962. A year later, another Soviet commentator conceded that the Common Market was ahead of CEMA in specialization of production, an area in which the communist economists had claimed the particular advantage of the socialist system. See I. Ivanov, " 'The Common Market' and the Competition of the Two Systems," *Mirovaia Ekonomika i Mezhdunarodnye Otnosheniia*, No. 7 (July, 1963). A more optimistic assessment of communist economic integration is to be found in I. Dudinsky, "Economic Consolidation of Socialist States and European Integration," *Mirovaia Ekonomika i Mezhdunarodnye Otnosheniia*, No. 12 (December, 1962), pp. 3–15.

34. "The Co-operation of Socialist Countries Is Strengthening," *Kommunist*, June, 1962.

35. Senin, *op. cit.*

36. I. Rachmuth, "The Importance of Establishing a Rate of Development Which Will Level Off the Economic Progress of All Socialist Countries," *Probleme Economice*, July, 1963.

37. Ivanov, *op. cit.*

38. This assertion, factually quite true, had a special irony. A Soviet writer, Mel'nikov, writing almost simultaneously in Moscow, made much of the point that uneven indexes of industrial development in the West proved the correctness of "the law of uneven development of capitalism, discovered by Lenin." The table below combines the Rumanian's data for the East with Soviet statistics for the West:

INDUSTRIAL PRODUCTION

	1950*	1960	1962
Italy	100	230	280
West Germany	100	249	276
France	100	187	209
Rumania	100	340	448
Czechoslovakia	100	281	325
East Germany	100	292	330

* The base year.

Thus, it is quite striking that the "law . . . discovered by Lenin" had at least as much applicability to the Communist countries. D. Mel'nikov, "The Sharpening of Imperialist Contradictions in the Contemporary Phase," *Mirovaia Ekonomika i Mezhdunarodnye Otnosheniia*, No. 6, 1963, and Rachmuth, *op. cit.*; statistics for the West from the Special Appendix to *Mirovaia Ekonomika i Mezhdunarodnye Otnosheniia*, No. 8, 1963: "Ekonomicheskoe Polozhenie Kapitalisticheskih Stran," page 5.

39. Rachmuth, *op. cit.*

40. Compare a Polish statement (by S. Kuzinski, "Concerning the International Socialist Division of Labor," *Nowe Drogi*, September, 1963) urging that a distinction be made between the immediate and the long range, and that during the former phase, internal, national needs be recognized, while later, the international criterion of efficiency might become dominant, with two contemporary Soviet statements, one seeming to accept some compromise on this issue (V. Terekhov and V. Shastitko, "The International Socialist Division of Labor—the Criteria of Efficiency," *Mirovaia Ekonomika i Mezhdunarodyne Otnosheniia*, No. 7, 1963), and the other attacking the idea of developing complex industries "within the framework of a closed national economy, particularly of a small country" (I. Dudinsky, "Strengthening the Economic Co-operation of Fraternal Countries," *Kommunist*, No. 12, August, 1963).

41. Khrushchev in *Kommunist*, *op. cit.*

42. A neat and useful summary is contained in S. Hoffmann, "De Gaulle, L'Europe, L'Alliance," *La Caravelle* (Boston), Spring, 1963.

43. See De Gaulle's speech in Lyons, September 28, 1963.

44. Press conference of July 29, 1963.

45. Press conference of March 25, 1959.

46. Some Gaullist spokesmen have projected this process even further. Jacques de Montalais (*Le Monde*, August 22, 1962) sees the following outcome: "Europe would extend southward through Africa and eastward through Siberia; the United States would extend northward through Canada and southward through Latin America; and finally China."

47. De Gaulle press conference, March 25, 1959: "The reunification of the two parts into a single Germany which would be entirely free seems to us the

normal destiny of the German people, *provided they do not re-open the question of their present frontiers to the west, the east, the north and the south,* and that they move toward integrating themselves one day in a contractual organization of all Europe for co-operation, liberty, and peace" (italics added).

48. A perceptive summary of the thrust of De Gaulle's Eastern policy is in A. Kawalkowski, "Alternatywa," *Kultura* (Paris), No. 9, 1962.

49. To perceive that this is not entirely unrealistic it is necessary only to remind oneself of the Strauss- von and zu Guttenberg alternative to the Shroeder line, or the revealing press conference of the German defense minister, Kai-Uwe von Hassel, on June 13, 1963, in which he came close to echoing the De Gaulle position.

50. This was in line with the thesis of inherent Franco-American economic contradictions. See V. Liubimova, "The Problems of France's Participation in the 'Common Market,'" *Mirovaia Ekonomika i Mezhdunarodnye Otnosheniia*, No. 3 (1957).

51. See note of Bulganin to Guy Mollet, May 21, 1957; and Khrushchev's statement to a *Figaro* correspondent, quoted in A. Manfred, "Franco-Soviet Relations," *International Affairs*, December, 1959.

52. *Pravda*, April 24, 1959.

53. Speech of October 31, 1959, and report to Muscovites on return from Paris on April 4, 1960.

54. For a detailed treatment, see G. Chernikov, "Economic Collaboration between France and the U.S.S.R.: Traditions and Perspectives," *Mirovaia Ekonomika i Mezhdunarodnye Otnosheniia*, No. 3, 1960, pp. 15–28.

55. *Pravda*, September 22, 1958.

56. "Chancellor Adenauer and Premier de Gaulle were concerned even at their first meeting not only with reaching agreement on their actions within their own countries but, it seems, also with how to draw the countries of Eastern Europe into the so-called European federation, which is nothing but a branch of the aggressive North Atlantic bloc."—*Pravda*, September 24, 1948.

57. *Izvestia*, September 11, 1960, commenting on De Gaulle's press conference of September 5, spoke of "plans hatched in Paris for French hegemony in Western Europe."

58. Khrushchev's report to the Soviet people after the Vienna meeting with Kennedy, *Pravda*, June 16, 1961.

59. *Izvestia*, July 14, 1961, commenting on De Gaulle's speech.

60. *Ibid.*, April 3, 1962, commenting on Franco-Soviet relations.

61. Official Soviet statement on the Franco-German entente, *Pravda*, September 19, 1962.

62. For example, see "The Imperialist Bloc Is Fast Disintegrating," *Jen Min Jih Pao*, February 24, 1963.

Notes on Contributors

ZBIGNIEW K. BRZEZINSKI, Director of the Research Institute on Communist Affairs and Professor of Public Law and Government at Columbia University, is the author of *The Soviet Bloc; Political Power: USA/USSR; Ideology and Power in Soviet Politics;* and numerous other books and articles.

JEAN-JACQUES DEMOREST, Chairman of the Department of Romance Literature, Cornell University, is the author of a war novel, *Les Passionnés ont vécu,* and of several literary studies on Pascal (*Dans Pascal; Pascal écrivain;* etc.). He served in the Free French forces and has been an adviser to the Ministry of National Education of the present French government.

WILLIAM DIEBOLD, JR., Senior Research Fellow at the Council on Foreign Relations in New York, is the author of *Trade and Payments in Western Europe; The Schuman Plan;* and numerous articles and studies.

SYDNEY N. FISHER, Co-ordinator of the Graduate Institute for World Affairs and Professor of History at Ohio State University, was editor of the *Middle East Journal,* and is the author and editor of numerous books and collections.

CARL H. FULDA, Professor of Law at the University of Texas, is the author of *Competition in the Regulated Industries: Transportation,* and numerous articles in various law journals on different aspects of the European Economic Community.

KLAUS KNORR, Director of the Center of International Studies and Professor of Economics at Princeton University, is the author of *The War Potential of Nations; NATO and American Security; Limited Strategic War;* and numerous articles for scholarly journals.

PAUL G. MINNEMAN, Agricultural Attaché at the American Embassy in Bonn, received his Ph.D. in Agricultural Economics at Ohio State University, and has served as Agricultural Attaché and Economic Counselor in Havana, Bern, Mexico City, London, Bucharest, Madrid, and Paris.

NORMAN J. G. POUNDS, Professor and Chairman of the Department of Geography at Indiana University, is the author of many books, including *The Ruhr, The Economic Pattern of Germany,* and, with William N. Parker, *Coal and Steel in Western Europe.* He has lectured at many universities and served as Lecturer in Geography at Clare College, Christ's College, and Fitzwilliam House at the University of Cambridge.

HANS A. SCHMITT, Professor of History at Tulane University, is the author of *The Path to European Union: From the Marshall Plan to the Common Market,* and numerous other works and articles on modern France and Germany.

170

Index